UNUSUAL
SHOPPING
IN PARIS

Our thanks to:

Emilie de Beaumont, Florent Billioud, Xinnan et Sébastien Billioud, Antoine Blachez, Philippe Bonfils, Ludovic Bonneton, Christine and André Bonneton, Louis-Marie Bourgeois, Etienne Darroman, Stéphane Decaux, Jérome Denoix, Anne Esambert, Vincent Formery, Oliver Gallmeister, Francois-Régis Gaudry, Cyrille George, Azmina Goulamaly, Romaine Guérin, Elvire Haberman, Aliette Jalenques, Antoine Jonglez, Aurélie Jonglez, Guillaume Jonglez, Timothée Jonglez, Frédéric Jousset, Stéphanie Kergall, Benoît de La Chapelle, Benoît de Larouzière, Oriane du Laurent, Xavier Lefranc, Emmanuel Legrand, Anne-Claire Levêque, Sophie and Xavier Lièvre, Jérome Lion, Lara de Nattes, Sophie Mazet, Suraj Natwani, Pauline and Lucas d'Orgeval, Marianne Perraut-Saussine, Francois and Sally Picard, Valérie Renaud, Adélaïde de Rendinger, Suzanne "Chick" du Rotrou, Pierre Santoul, Hervé Schlosser, Damien Seyriex, Ambroise Tézenas, Delphine and Nicolas Valluet, Marie-Aude and Kees Van Beek, Henri and Natacha Villeroy.

All too often, finding a birthday or Christmas present is a nightmare. Seized with last-minute panic, you end up buying any old thing, trampled by the frenzied crowds all with the same aim in mind.

To avoid such jams, we've taken great pleasure in drawing up this guide. So that shopping is no longer an ordeal, we've chosen a hundred or so places that are either very unusual in themselves or offer different, remarkable, and original products.

We hope that by following this guide you'll enjoy your shopping expeditions as much as we did, and that your presents will intrigue their recipients.

The guide is obviously not exhaustive. If you know of a product or service or a particularly unusual establishment that isn't mentioned, don't hesitate to let us know and we'll test it out for possible inclusion in a future edition.

Don't hesitate to write us:
By E-mail: info@editionsjonglez.com
By post: Editions Jonglez – 17, boulevard du Roi
78000 Versailles

MAIN PLACES

THEMES

COMME DES GARÇONS

54, rue du Faubourg-Saint-Honoré 75001 Paris
• Métro: Concorde or Madeleine
• Tel: 01 53 30 27 27
• Open Monday to Saturday 11.00–19.00

*A marvel
of beautiful
design*

Established in 2001, Comme des Garçons occupies a red-and-white townhouse that is a marvel of beautiful design. From the street there is almost no indication that the high-fashion store is inside. You need to go through into the inner courtyard to gain access to a venue based on a concept that will probably disconcert some customers.

To the left, one discovers a sublime room entirely decorated in red and furnished with cubic stools. There's nothing here for sale, however, customers are merely meant to spend time here, have a rest, or even meditate. When the machinery is switched on, some of the cubes begin to spin round, or move backwards and forwards.

If it's not working, just ask at the reception desk. For those who can't seem

to find the actual store entrance (and it seems that many have to retrace their steps!), it's located opposite the meditating space, right next to the glass doors: the red wall will slide back of its own accord …

Once inside this "pavilion", the visitor can soak up the ambiance created by the talented minds at work for the Japanese fashion label, Rei Kawakubo. Sliding room dividers and low furniture, walls and fittings covered with shiny glass fibre. You'd think you were anywhere but in a shop. The architect responsible is Takao Kawasaki.

For both men and women, the garments and accessories are a mix of styles: dresses, jackets, shirts, jumpers, T-shirts, sneakers, ankle boots. From classics to original designs.

COUTANCIE BEEF FROM LA BOUCHERIE BARONE

6, rue du Marché-Saint-Honoré 75001 Paris
• Métro: Tuileries or Pyramides
• Tel: 01 42 61 01 77
• Open Tuesday to Saturday 9.00–13.00 and 16.00–19.30
• E-mail: gbarone@noos.fr (no website)

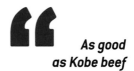

As good as Kobe beef

Tucked away in the city centre, among the offices and top fashion houses, the tiny Barone butcher's shop offers some of the finest meat in Paris, notably the famous Coutancie beef. Raised according to the traditional methods of Limousin farmers, the Limousin and Blonde d'Aquitaine cattle from which this very high quality meat is produced have been fed on exclusively natural foodstuffs from the meadows of the Périgord Vert countryside. Housed in comfortable stalls, they receive special care. At one time, these lucky beasts were even massaged twice a day …

Like the celebrated Kobe beef cattle of Japan, Coutancie cattle get a daily ration of fermented corn (5 kilos a day), which replaces the 3 litres of beer that they were formerly given. The alcohol in the feed improves the animals' appetites, encouraging marbling of the meat and giving it that inimitable flavour, tender, healthy and natural!

Barone's is a family business: in 1975, the parents installed themselves in this wonderful establishment. Then in 1990, it was the turn of their son Gilles to choose the products and welcome the customers: mostly local people from the neighbourhood but also those who, between business meetings, make a detour to this haven of authenticity to buy a Challosse or Coutancie beef rib, a géline de Touraine (€11.80 a kilo), a Kerguilavant chicken (€8 a kilo), or perhaps some belly pork fermier d'Auvergne.

The top quality meat sold here, which has won a multitude of prizes and medals, is tasty and chosen with great care. It won't even cost you more than elsewhere in Paris: about €26.50 a kilo for a faux-filet of Coutancie beef, perfectly marbled, smooth-textured and supple, ruby-red and gleaming …

OTHER BUTCHERS SELLING COUTANCIE BEEF:

BOUCHERIE DU CENTRE
6, rue Bouchut 75015 Paris
• Métro Ségur or Sèvres-Lecourbe
• Tel: 01 47 83 73 86
• Open Monday to Friday 7.00–13.00 and 16.00–20.00 and Saturday 7.00–14.00

LAFAYETTE GOURMET
48, boulevard Haussmann 75009 Paris
• Métro Chaussée-d'Antin or RER Auber
• Tel: 01 40 23 52 80
• Open Monday to Saturday 8.30–19.30, Thursday evening until 21.00

L'ATELIER MÉDICAL

61, rue des Petits-Champs 75001 Paris
• Métro: Pyramides, Opéra or Quatre-Septembre
• Tel: 01 42 60 20 20
• Ground floor, rear of courtyard
• Open Monday, Tuesday, Thursday 9.00–18.30, Wednesday 9.00–13.0 and
  Friday 9.00–17.00

A very charming doctor's surgery

I f you're put off by the idea of visiting a doctor in a white and sterile clinic or whose waiting room is grey and dusty, push open the blue door of an 18th-century building in rue des Petits-Champs, near the Palais Royal.

At the rear of the courtyard is a flower-bedecked workshop with a beautiful large glass roof. Despite appearances this is neither a guest house nor a tea-shop, and still less an interior decorating store, but rather a doctor's surgery specializing in laser treatments.

The chief doctor, Vincent Lecocq, a voluble and charming slender forty-something, explains that he once asked his children – he has nine! – to describe the typical waiting room of a hospital or clinic: "cold, white, straight lines, old magazines lying around, a pathetic poster on the wall …". Following these remarks, Vincent Lecocq and his assistant, doctor Valérie Leduc, phlebologist [vein specialist], chose to receive their patients in a radically different atmosphere: full of light, comfortable and welcoming.

Under the soft light diffused by the glass roof, beige, white and grey blend in with pale wood. Small armchairs, just like at home, coffee-table books, bunches of flowers, pictures and countless clocks on the walls. It is said that the place was occupied for a long time by a clock workshop. True or not, the timepieces are there to remind us that punctuality is all and that passing time also marks the faces of the patients who come in for a photorajeunissement (rejuvenating treatment, €150), or treatment for sun damage and broken veins (€120–€150).

In this charmingly offbeat surgery, which nevertheless uses ultra-sophisticated equipment, women no longer have any excuse for not getting rid of unwanted hair, blemishes and other vein problems once and for all …

BACQUEVILLE

6-7-8, galerie Montpensier - Jardin du Palais-Royal 75001 Paris
- Métro: Pyramides or Palais-Royal
- Tel: 01 42 96 26 90
- Open Monday to Friday 9.30–18.00
- www.bacqueville.com

Anybody can buy a légion d'honneur, but you need proof to wear one...

No need for your name to be in the reports to be decorated for bravery. At Bacqueville, anybody can buy a decoration like the légion d'honneur. But to wear the medal in public you'll need an official attestation that you earned it. Meanwhile, pop along to the Palais Royal to pick out your model. The choice is yours: chevalier, officier or commandeur. It'll be made from brass (€47) as only authentic holders have the right to order their decorations in precious metals.

That is in fact the main source of business for this well-placed outlet, since 1790 one of the rare establishments in France to have the right to cast medals. Their workshop is on the outskirts of Paris.

The Bacqueville family founded this 200-year-old shop selling official decorations, before ceding it only a few years ago to another family, the Marks. While enjoying the view over one of the most ravishing Parisian gardens, you can browse through the thousands of ribbons, cockades, municipal sashes, barrettes and other insignia. Medal of the Ordre National du Mérite, Ordre des Arts et Lettres, Ordre du Mérite Agricole ... You might also glimpse plenty of celebrities here. But the decoration most often requested is none other than the Médaille du Travail [Workers Medal]. Bacqueville has made 70,000 of them for clients including all the major French companies, from Darty to Renault. This medal costs as little as €10, in silver gilt. In solid silver, it will set you back around €30.

OTHER SHOPS SELLING MEDALS AND DECORATIONS:

MARIE STUART
3, galerie Montpensier 75001 Paris
- Tel: 01 42 96 20 25

LA MONNAIE DE PARIS
11, quai Conti 75006 Paris
- Tel: 01 40 46 58 50

ARTHUS BERTRAND
6, place Saint-Germain-des-Prés 75006 Paris
- Tel: 01 43 54 72 10

WAAF ET MIAOU

14, avenue de l'Opéra 75001 Paris
• Métro: Pyramides
• Tel: 01 42 60 02 26
• Fax: 01 42 60 02 47
• Open Monday to Friday 10.00–20.00,
  Sundays and public holidays 13.00–20.00

Dress your dog as Father Christmas

Clothes shops for dogs are in fashion, Paris is full of them. This one however takes the concept further than the others …

Although you'll find the usual denim jackets, woolly jumpers, tweed coats, frilly dresses, rainwear, anoraks, T-shirts and vests here, you can also buy less traditional accessories: angels' wings, Father Christmas outfits, sunglasses, bow-ties, material for duvets, baseball caps …

Rummage through the shelves and you'll come across other marvels. Staunch fans of animal outfits shouldn't hesitate to have a good look round! Some joys not to be missed include an entire drawer at the back of the shop reserved for garments imported from Japan. In there, we dug out a classy outfit for a chihuahua (Paris Hilton wouldn't say no for Tinkerbell). Of course the shop is owned by a Japanese woman, Mitsuko, with a Westie who likes to have her photo taken, provided she isn't dressed up as Maya l'abeille* …

*Maya l'abeille (Mitsubachi Maya no bôken) is an Australian/Japanese cartoon series created in 1975 by Nisan Takahashi based on a story by Waldemar Bonsels, which has also been shown on French TV.

FULL MOON LEGENDS

Popular beliefs associate a number of occurrences with the night of the full moon. Apart from making your hair grow faster, pushing criminals into gratifying their impulses (people with mental illness find their symptoms get worse), or giving those with suicidal tendencies the courage to do away with themselves, other legends exist.

For example, more births are supposed to take place (scientific studies in fact show this to be statistically false), and certain gardening jobs (cuttings, grafts, etc.) are said to benefit, which is quite possible because the full moon gives off a considerable amount of luminous energy. Some people even plant seeds only when the moon is waxing and roots when it is waning...

Surfaces exposed to moonlight are also thought to grow shinier. At least that's the claim put forward by Berluti, the famous luxury footwear manufacturer: made-to-measure shoes are laid out in the rays of the waxing moon to acquire their legendary patina.

MAACHI DJELANI

40, rue Coquillière 75001 Paris
- Métro: Les Halles
- Tel/Fax: 01 42 33 57 47
- Open daily 10.00–20.00 and all night when the moon is full
- www.lookmachine.com

Hairdresser of the full moon

On nights when the moon is full, curious night birds who've managed to avoid the effects of alcohol or other illicit substances may be surprised to see people getting their hair cut at 4 or 5 in the morning.

In his ultracool hairdressing salon near Les Halles, Djelani Maachi is actually practising an old belief that hair grows back faster when the moon is full (and more slowly the next day). "Hair can grow as much as 2.5 cm instead of the usual one centimetre per month," he says. One tends to believe him, and if you need further convincing, just go along to the salon one night when the moon is full.

While the street sleeps, Monsieur Maachi, scissors and comb in hand, cuts steadily through the early hours. His clientele come from all over: "Sometimes I don't close all night", claims the hairdresser.

Recently, our friend Maachi, who also does hair for celebrities, took a gamble on another idea to make his business viable during the day – the relookage [make-over]. "I was the first hairdresser to use information technology." So his salon looks more like a film studio with its computers and plasma screen. Starting from a simple photo and applying powerful software, he gives you a whole new look based on the resulting picture.

RATS SURMULOTS
(RATS D'ÉGOUTS)
CAPTURÉS AUX HALLES
VERS 1925

DEAD RATS IN THE WINDOW MAISON AUROUZE

8, rue des Halles 75001 Paris
- Métro: Châtelet
- Tel: 01 40 41 16 20
- Fax: 01 40 41 16 21
- Open Monday to Friday 9.00–12.30 and 14.00–18.30, Saturday 9.00–12.30 and 14.00–18.00
- www.aurouze.fr

Generations of rodent catchers

Rodent catchers, now there's a niche market that does everybody a favour, including tourists, who gleefully admire the fine collection of dead rats hanging in the window. Maison Aurouze still has its premises in Les Halles, where it has been since 1872 ... Over the shop window, a sign proclaims "Destruction of vermin", and rightly so: no crawling or flying pest can resist this family. "Ratters" from father to son, they also mix their own (miraculous!) concoctions that eliminate cockroaches and other undesirable intruders. Prices start at €1.20, for a mousetrap.

SIGHTS NEARBY

VACHE AND COW
12, rue de la Ferronnerie 75001 Paris
- Métro: Châtelet
- Tel: 01 40 26 60 36
- Open Monday 13.00–19.00 and Tuesday to Saturday 11.00–19.00
- www.vacheandcow.com

With its wooden shop front and its "life-sized" cows keeping watch, Vache and Cow looks rather like a stable. Entirely devoted to the cow, this shop offers nearly 1,400 different bovine effigies, ranging from salt cellars to ashtrays, without forgetting the hat, the garden gnome or even the car dustcover. There's something here for everybody. Fans of contemporary art won't feel left out once they see the large selection of miniature cow figures copied from the Cow Parade (an urban event where life-sized cows decorated by contemporary artists invade the streets of the world's great cities).

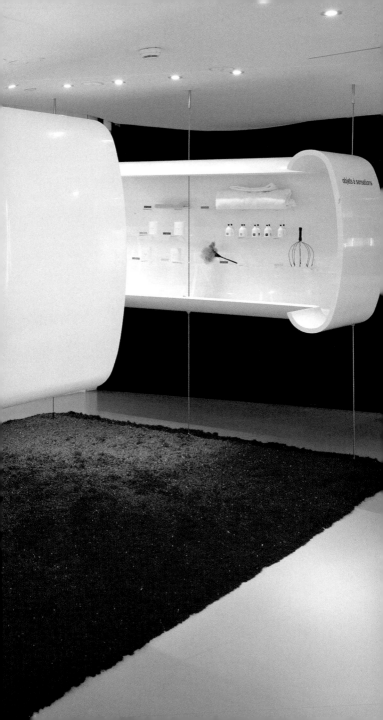

LA BULLE KENZO

1, rue du Pont-Neuf 75001 Paris
- Métro: Pont-Neuf
- Tel: 01 73 04 20 04
- Open Monday to Saturday 10.00—20.00
- www.labullekenzo.com

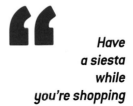

Have a siesta while you're shopping

Perched on the fourth floor of the Kenzo building at Pont Neuf, La Bulle Kenzo is a timeless place, intended to bowl you over, or at least make your senses more acute. Very clinical, done out almost entirely in white brightened with occasional touches of colour, this shop mainly sells the Kenzo line of beauty products. But you'll also find perfume, candles, all kinds of cuddly toys, T-shirts to die for (little windows open to show off your skin) and other sensual objects: voodoolove, sensational sweeties, marshmallow necklaces …

Apart from the playful nature of some of these objects, the "bubble" boasts an amazing and original interior design: at the back of the room stand two white bubbles, one of them covered in plastic hair, containing massage salons bathed in yellow light. On the menu are treatments just as idiosyncratic as the setting: massage with candles and rice (?80), marshmallow massage (€70), or a face vitality treatment (€60). You can even have a siesta there (no appointment needed, €15): images, music, a good mattress and a gentle awakening …

PERSONALIZE YOUR KIDS' COMIC BOOKS
MOI, LE HÉROS
32, rue Montmartre 75002 Paris • Métro: Etienne-Marcel
• Tel: 01 42 21 07 17 • Open 11.00 -19.30 Tuesday to Saturday and
11.30– 19.30 Monday • www.moisheros.com

Offer children a story that features them in it. Thanks to "Moi, le Héros", little Jane or Johnny will see themselves transformed into leading characters in a printed book. The idea is so simple, why didn't we think of it! This specialist toy shop near Les Halles takes orders for children's books in which the details of the story's hero (me) are made to measure. Thus you can use the first name, age and home town of the child the book is intended for. Likewise for two other children who accompany the hero and one adult. You can't change the storyline itself, however. There are two alternatives, suitable for different age groups: Top Secret (up to 10 years.) and Ulunla (up to 6 years). Best of all, your dedication and the date the book was ordered will be printed on the first page. Allow a month and a half maximum for delivery. A book costs €25.

ELVIS MY HAPPINESS

9, rue Notre-Dame-des-Victoires 75002 Paris
- Métro: Bourse
- Tel: 01 49 27 08 43
- Fax: 01 49 27 08 40
- Open Monday to Saturday 10.30–13.00 and 14.30–19.00

*Dedicated
to the cult
of the King*

À short distance from place des Victoires, members of the faith with a shared passion for Elvis Presley meet regularly in what is probably the only shop in Europe dedicated to the King, according to the owner. He also claims that Elvis is the only artist to have his own shop in France. Some people would give their right arm to possess one of "his" garments (even a pair of glasses that belonged to him sells for €38,000). Others have lost count of their plane journeys to the annual gathering at Graceland (for August 2007, which will mark the thirtieth anniversary of his passing, the hotels are already full).

More moderate fans, however, may content themselves with an Elvis head dangling from their rearview mirror …

As far as unusual objects go, the shop is a treasure trove: a set of coffee spoons in the shape of the King's guitar (€12 each), earrings with the illustrious name (€23), small photos for €2 (Elvis as a cowboy, Elvis in spangled costume, Elvis in a kimono, Elvis in the army …) and a black tank top with red trim marked Elvis (€38).

Music lovers aren't forgotten. A splendid selection of records and CDs, including some collector's items, is available. Plus the usual DVDs, posters, statuettes and other kitsch items.

MARTIN GRANT

10, rue Charlot 75003 Paris
- Métro: Arts-et-Métiers or Filles-du-Calvaire
- 2nd floor, right-hand door
- Tel: 01 42 71 39 49
- Open Monday to Friday 10.00–18.00
- www.martingrantparis.com

Young designer at home

Located quite simply in the designer's personal flat (together with the workshop and offices), and only indicated by a nameplate without opening hours or a phone number, Martin Grant's shop isn't easy to find.

Once you've got over the surprise of ringing someone's doorbell, you'll receive a very courteous welcome. The shop itself consists of a small room with a bare wooden floor. Along the left-hand wall, one finds the spring collection for sale.

On the clothes rack covering the right-hand wall is the next collection, not yet on sale.

You're allowed to look around for a few minutes, then an assistant comes back and asks if you need anything. The garments themselves are cut from very beautiful natural materials (a lot of taffeta, wool and cotton), in a style that is almost monastic in its simplicity and yet the epitome of Parisian elegance.

You'll soon want to try everything on!

Based in Paris for some 15 years now, Martin Grant, whose work is much better known abroad than in France, previously occupied a streetfront shop in the Marais before choosing confidentiality and word-of-mouth as a marketing strategy. In this way the customer's needs are better catered for: if you like one of the styles but prefer blue rather than beige, no problem! But watch out, once you fasten your eye on the coats you'll be tempted to buy them all ... Prices range from €500 to €800 for a dress, €1,000 to €1,600 for a coat.

ROBOPOLIS - LA BOUTIQUE DES ROBOTS

107, boulevard Beaumarchais 75003 Paris
- Métro: Saint-Sébastien
- Tel: 01 44 78 01 18
- Open Tuesday to Saturday 10.00–19.30

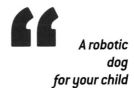

*A robotic
dog
for your child*

An end to that most dreadful of household chores the robot vacuum cleaner is here. The sweetly named Roomba is shaped like an ice hockey puck, only larger. It has been selling for a few years now and is still undergoing improvements, the latest version supposedly always more efficient.

Fortunately, it's simple to use – the least you could expect given the price (€399). It works like this: place your new cleaner in the middle of the room, where it'll start going round in circles. It's intelligent and will even pass under the bed and your other furniture, without falling down the stairs.

A word of warning to cat and dog owners: nothing resists Roomba, not even animal hair. Once the cleaning is finished, Roomba returns quietly to its stand to recharge its batteries. Fanatics can always use the remote control to make it go over the room again once or twice, sending it into the corners just to annoy it.

Open since 2003, Robopolis is also the only place in France where you can buy Sony's famous robot dog, Aibo. At the rear of the shop, the strange object gives a permanent demonstration, except when he's resting. You'll see Aibo taking photos, speaking English, and putting his toys away. He is completely useless and thus very expensive (€2,099). But he doesn't shed hair and does not need to be taken out three times a day. That alone is worth a lot.

NABAZTAG, THE TALKING RABBIT

Haven't you heard of Nabaztag yet? The incredible white rabbit (€95) works on your Wifi network: remote controlled over the internet, he'll speak, play music, and murmur sweet nothings upon request. All you have to do is log on to the website www.nabaztag.com and send your message to your friend's, lover's or brother's rabbit € So now you can wake them up in the middle of the night by having the rabbit in their bedroom shout: "I think you make a very nice couple." To get the most fun out of this, supply all the members of your tribe with one. Guaranteed madness. Not only will it get you out of bed in the morning, keep you up to date on your stocks and shares, announce the temperature and the air pollution rate, your Nabaztag can also carry on remote conversations with your associates.
A French invention, Nabaztag can be found at Fnac, Chez Colette, Robopolis (see above) and also at Nem (67, rue de Richelieu – Tel: 01 40 20 06 09).

CANICRÈCHE

32, rue de Turbigo 75003 Paris
• Métro: Etienne-Marcel
• Tel: 01 42 71 59 09
• Open Monday to Saturday 8.00–20.00
• www.canicreche.fr
• €7 per hour (digressive hourly rate)

*The first
crèche
for dogs*

I n May 2005 the first crèche for dogs opened in Paris, near Beaubourg. Although
the principle of "Dog Day Care" has exis-
ted since time immemorial on the other
side of the Atlantic, the idea had never taken
off in France, despite the large dog population in the capital. So the market
was there: the doggies, used to lounging about in their kennels, could at last
be let loose and their guilty owners could put their minds at rest …

Just as for children, this Canicrèche is designed so that the happy guests can
make the most of themselves in a large and appropriate space, following a
schedule carefully worked out by a specialist trained at Maison-Alfort vete-
rinary school and helped by several staff.

There's a full daily programme. A sporting session takes place in the "gym"
on the ground floor, with an obstacle course (tyre, tunnel) designed to stret-
ch the legs. But there are also three 20-minute walks per day and pauses for
a nap in the basement, which has been divided into several compartments
so that everyone has their own room.

As for food, the house does guests proud, although those there just for the
day have to bring their own pâté. Since the stomachs of our four-legged
friends are delicate, "the dog gets exactly the same food and brand of biscuits that it's used to at home." The owner of the establishment has been
known to get busy in the kitchen preparing chicken breast with carrots and
veal escalope with green beans when required …

AN ETERNALLY EPHEMERAL BOUTIQUE
WHITE SHOP
82, rue des Gravilliers 75003 Paris • Métro: Arts-et-Métiers
• Tel: 01 42 76 04 04 • Open 13.00–20.00

Welcome to the world of the ephemeral. White Shop is a short-lived retail outlet
that changes even its name every month, if not every week.
The team at Blast, a trendy Parisian magazine, launched the new concept in late
2005 by opening this shop, tucked away in a small street a few steps from
Centre Georges Pompidou.
The space, rather cramped but well designed, is taken over for a limited time by
all kinds of products to be presented to the chance new "members" of the club.
Obviously you have to join to be a member. Once a month the club organises
soirées, notably for the opening of the new boutique. Otherwise, anyone attending
the openings can still buy something or just hang around …

HANDS AND FEET - BRIGITTE MASSOUTIER

22, passage Molière 75003 Paris
- Métro: Rambuteau
- Tel: 01 42 77 53 50
- Open Friday and Saturday 14.00—18.00

*Have
a cast made
of your hand or foot*

The body is her business. In the enchanting passage Molière, Brigitte Massoutier makes casts of feet and hands, but also ears, breasts and bums. Her favourite working material, plâtre-pierre ["stone-plaster"], doesn't erode and lasts a lifetime. It is thus an incredible idea for a three-dimensional souvenir present.

The procedure is simple and not very demanding. "The most difficult thing about it is singing to put the model at ease," jokes Brigitte Massoutier. The artist takes the impression in a few minutes, preferably in her workshop, and delivers the cast around a month later.

One of Brigitte's really good ideas was to go into maternity hospitals on request to make casts, based on alginate and warm water, of the feet and hands of new babies. Her youngest model was 57 minutes old.

But she obviously also has adult customers: the oldest woman was 98 at the time the impression was taken.

The results are indeed… impressive: each cast of a hand faithfully reproduces the fingerprints. Prices are €150 for a baby's hand or foot and around €250 for an adult hand. Those who can't afford that can try doing it themselves: it's very easy (see below), much cheaper, and guaranteed fun with close friends at hand… or foot. It might also be a good opportunity to offer an original wedding present. After a few trial runs, go wild: cast the hands of a few people (three or four is ideal), buy a large and attractive piece of wood, borrow a drill from your favourite engineer (bound to have one), attach the hands onto the wood, and you'll have a superb coat-rack and a lifelong memento of your friends …

THE EASY WAY TO MAKE YOUR OWN CASTS

Buy some alginate at Graphigro (three outlets in Paris) or Adam at Montparnasse for the "negative". Follow the instructions for use: prepare the mould, slip your hand (for example) inside and wait a few minutes. Take your hand out (the alginate stretches slightly) and the mould is ready. Pour in plaster or resin, which you can buy at the same place. Wait a few minutes, break the mould (which is only used once) and your hand is ready.

SAADETIAN

18, rue de Picardie 75003 Paris
- Métro: Temple or Republique
- Tel: 01 48 87 99 06
- Open Tuesday to Saturday 13.30–18.30
- www.saadetian.com

A living museum of traditional dress

Now one of the few manufacturers of hunting outfits in France (as well as other hard-to-find civilian and military clothing), Monsieur Saadetian, tailor by trade, like his father before him, also designs and makes uniforms for the Order of the Knights of Malta.

His cluttered workshop is housed in an unimaginably decrepit old building. This veritable living museum of traditional dress has a very homely atmosphere.

Although you may not find treasures from another age there, you'll learn a lot more about the history of costume than from any encyclopaedia, thanks to loquacity of the owner, sometimes joined by his equally pleasant elderly mother.

Nothing strange about that: the family has run the business since 1926. Of Armenian origin, Saadetian's grandfather started off by manufacturing military kit, which led to his becoming acquainted with hunting circles. The workshop thus became to all intents and purposes the official suppliers to the members of a number of hunting bodies. Their made-to-measure jackets require 45 hours of work.

Although foxhunting is now frequently opposed (it has for example recently been banned in the UK), Monsieur Saadetian is still in the game. His business has even tended to expand with the various restrictions on hunting in Europe, France having become one of the last bastions of this noble pursuit.

Daniel Saadetian is also a mine of anecdotes on the traditions of hunting with hounds and the characteristics of hunting packs. A world that is sometimes just as closed as the doors of his little shop are wide open.

MADEMOISELLE ROSE CRÉATION

4, rue Fontaine du Temple 75003 Paris
- 2nd floor
- Métro: Temple or République
- Tel: 01 48 04 55 59
- By appointment only
- www.mademoisellerose.com
- From €110 to €170 for a white or light ivory pair - Supplement €50 euros
  for single shade, €75 for two-tone
  Individual estimates for accessories

*Buying
shoes
in a flat*

Mademoiselle Rose, a leading figure in Lyonnaise elegance, set up this Paris showroom at the beginning of 2006 to display her latest creations in footwear and handbags.

To receive her exclusively female clientele, she chose a flat with character which she then transformed into a modern boudoir. The result is a great success: the spaces are pleasant, the decor both refined and warm, bringing out the best in the selection of shoes on display. But there's another important detail: service is personalized, with two private advisers, Catherine and Julien, receiving individual customers by appointment.

The guiding principle is simple: from over forty different styles, all made from satin lined with natural leather, you pick the one that best suits your current mood.

Whether they are evening high heels or shoes for everyday use, Mademoiselle Rose's teams then take charge of matching them to the colour of your outfit or customizing them according to your wishes, however fanciful they may be. All

shades are available and the shoes can be finished with a range of accessories: feathers, paste gems, lace, etc. Some highly unusual models have come out of her workshops, such as a pair of shoes entirely covered with Swarovski crystals. Today, the creativity and technique of Mademoiselle Rose have received the recognition they deserve: the Lyonnais couturier Nicolas Fafiotte called on her talents in putting the finishing touches to the outfits worn by Miss France finalists.

ALAIN, MASTER BARBER

8, rue Saint-Claude 75003 Paris
- Métro: Saint-Sébastien-Froissart
- Tel: 01 42 77 55 80
- Open Tuesday to Saturday 9.15–19.00

An old-fashioned close shave

Afar cry from the ranks of disposable supermarket razors, this haven for the hirsute in the Marais district of Paris has a suitably old-fashioned look. The proprietor is called Alain. Not only is he one of the last master barbers in the city, but also a charismatic personality happy to bring this vanishing, seldom-taught trade back into vogue.

The adventure starts on the pavement outside: rue Saint-Claude has the charm of those narrow alleyways that you can just picture as the setting for a 1950s film.

At the end of the street near boulevard Beaumarchais, one spies a lighted window. This is Alain's. Go in and let yourself soak up the atmosphere of the place.

On the walls are dozens of cut-throat razors, belonging to regular customers or celebrities (Johnny Hallyday has dropped in on occasion), interspersed with commemorative plates (some with instructive texts), scissors, and crimping irons (to shape the moustache). Alain wanted to make a mini museum of his salon in homage to the traditional shaving ritual, daily, or thrice weekly, which had been abandoned in France by the 1970s.

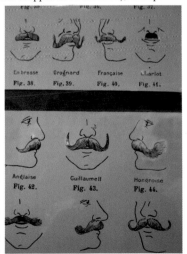

That said, don't expect to find a dust-covered dinosaur in his window. The place is smart. When he's not wielding the blade, the lively, genial and generous Alain will gladly fit you in between two other customers. The tools of his trade gleam like they would have done in the old days, as if Jean Gabin had just left the room.

k top = 5,90 €

k top = 10,50 €

Schweppes

top

LA BOUTIQUE DES INVENTIONS

13, rue Saint-Paul 75004 Paris
• Métro: Saint-Paul
• Tel: 01 42 71 44 19
• Open Wednesday to Sunday 11.00–19.00
• www.la-boutique-des-inventions.com

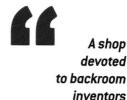

A shop devoted to backroom inventors

I sabelle Risacher's establishment is a shrine to the ordinary person's powers of imagination. The aim of this little shop, hidden in a out-of-the-way corner of the Marais, is to sell original and practical objects patented by their developers. So you may very well find here the thing you've always dreamed of but never come across before. Quite often, without anyone hearing about it, it turns out that somebody has already invented it … But most of the time, due to lack of funds to develop a prototype, the marvel never sees the light of day.

Isabelle Risacher thought of opening an outlet for such backroom inventors in 2001: she is committed to helping them perfect their products, especially by testing them on customers. On the shelves of the rue Saint-Paul shop you can therefore find some incredible things, sometimes strange, always astute, like a can sealer. Practical souls will be in seventh heaven: the tarte facile [easy pie] spreads pastry evenly in the baking dish (€20); the anticlaque porte [anti-door slammer], as its name suggests,

makes draughts less troublesome (€15 for two); the talonnière protects the heels of shoes while driving (€7). Tea-drinkers will love the kangaroo cup, with a pouch to put the teabag in when the brew is ready (€10). Even more ingenious, behold the tropiflore (€46): "a turntable, moving 6 cm every 2 hours, so that plants have maximum benefit from the light". Finally, why didn't we think of it before, a warning horn for skaters (€30). Blessed be its creator.

L'EMBELLIE

29, boulevard Henri-IV 75004 Paris
• Métro: Sully-Morland
• Tel: 01 42 74 36 33
• Open Tuesday to Saturday 11.00–19.00

Everything you might need on leaving hospital

In order to spare cancer patients having to search for the things they need, despite their fatigue, the founder of L'Embellie opened this pretty shop near the Bastille in April 2005. In a comfortable setting, the most unlikely purchases can be made calmly, quietly and even pleasantly.

As in a traditional gift shop, the welcome is both discreet and efficient, the decoration simple and warm.

But, on the shelves, the clothing and items on sale are aimed at specific needs. You'll find, for example, a wide range of wigs and head-coverings (€20.50–€80) for those who have lost their hair; anti-nausea bracelets; breast prostheses in as wide a choice as offered by specialists; eyebrow make-up kits (€34); bio-cosmetics for damaged skin, shawls and scarves for those feeling the cold; special bathing costumes for prosthetic limbs or dressing gowns that are easy to slip off. Also for sale is a range of publications on cancer as well as objects for the bedside table: photo frames, alarm clocks, sleeping masks, wash-bags, jewellery … In short, things to help reawaken a sense of femininity, or simply to feel better …

L'Embellie also organizes workshops to learn how to relax (relaxation therapy, yoga) or to talk about your illness (support groups). All at the most reasonable prices: €20 annual membership and €3 per workshop.

LA BOUTIQUE SENTIMENTALE

14, rue du Roi-de-Sicile 75004 Paris
• Métro: Saint-Paul
• Tel: 01 42 78 84 04
• Open Tuesday to Saturday 14.00–18.30, or mornings by appointment

Have your favourite shoes copied

This shop may look nondescript, yet in this simply decorated place Monsieur Boussi has no doubt performed an invaluable service to countless numbers of people. At least once in their life, everyone has had a favourite pair of shoes, rather like a second skin, impossible to throw out even when they're falling apart.

Since 1986, Monsieur Boussi has been making identical copies of shoes, in the material (preferably leather) and colour of your choice. At the outset, the craftsman launched a ready-to-wear range of footwgear but gradually shifted to made-to-measure. And not only fashion items: he has also made built-up shoes for a dwarf and regularly responds to requests for bride-grooms' styles. Lastly, he has a catalogue of his own designs, available to order in a number of colours for around €245.

To have a copy made, allow four weeks for the work. You'll need to leave the original pair with the craftsman and shell out between €360 and €460. Boots, slippers, high heels, sandals, brogues, ballet shoes … Monsieur Boussi insists that he can make anything, or almost anything.

Services of this type are often found in certain developing countries (notably India and South-East Asia), but as far as we know, this is the only one of its kind in Paris, apart from the JL Chaussures shop in the 20th arrondissement.

WILLY-SHAPED BAGUETTES
LE GAY CHOC
45, rue Sainte-Croix-la-Bretonnerie 75004 Paris
• Métro: Hôtel de Ville
• Tel: 01 48 87 56 88
• Open daily except Wednesday 9.00–20.30

To impress your friends when they're round to dinner, there's nothing like a baguette in the shape of a manly willy! Better tasting, obviously, they come in three sizes to suit your friends: small at €2.20, medium at €4.20 and large at €6.20… You'll be sure to find them on Saturday and Sunday, the man in the shop says.

LITCHI

4, rue des Écouffes 75004 Paris
- Métro: Saint-Paul
- Tel: 01 44 59 39 09
- Open Tuesday to Saturday 11.30–19.30, Sunday 13.30–19.30
- www.litchi.com

Sweets with a picture of the Pope

Litchi is located in the little rue des Écouffes, in the heart of the Marais. That's where you can find the famous giant lollipops bearing a photo of Jean-Paul II. "We had new stock delivered two days before the Pope's death," explains Aurore, the shopkeeper. "There are plenty left, but in any case I think we'll keep them in stock even if new ones with Benoît XVI's head also come out."

Since Litchi, open since September 2002, is the shop of "all world faiths, from a kitsch, naïve but sincere point of view", you'll also find Peruvian amulets, macho fetish objects, good-luck sprays, Brazilian charm bracelets, and Mexican amulets, alongside the more mainstream Buddhas and Holy Virgins …

The team of buyers from Paris travel widely, as well as having a dozen contacts based in the most productive countries: Brazil, Mexico, Peru, India, China and Japan. To be sure of covering everything, Litchi would like to import more from North African countries, which are equally well-endowed with religious paraphernalia.

HAVE YOUR CONDOMS DELIVERED
NÉMO
- www.23h-5h.com
- Tel: 01 47 00 43 32
- Deliveries from 1st to 11th arrondissements

When you're in the middle of action, you don't necessarily want to get dressed and go out to buy a packet of condoms at the corner shop. This ingenious home-delivery service offers packets of condoms (€4 for three) at any hour of the night, starting at 19.00 and finishing at 6.00 in the morning. Order just as you would a take-away, ring the service and wait a while. In less than 45 minutes the package will be delivered to your door.

GELATI D'ALBERTO

45, rue Mouffetard 75005 Paris
- Métro: Place-Monge or RER Luxembourg
- Tel: 01 77 11 44 55
- Open daily from April to end of November 12.00–00.30
- Other shop: 12, rue des Lombards 75004 Paris – Métro: Châtelet or Hôtel-de-Ville
  Here, you can view the laboratory taste the ice creams on the premises.
  Open all year round.

> **Rose-shaped
> ices**

Around rue Mouffetard you may be rather surprised to come across tourists and regulars busily eating a ravishing sorbet with a strawberry heart and mango petals … These happy strollers with beaming smiles on their faces have just come out of the little violet-coloured shop of master ice cream maker Alberto …

Bursting with life in clothes whose acid colours match the sorbets she sells, Jennifer can even make you an ice shaped like rose petals! To the sound of Latin music throughout the day and techno in the evening, the only problem is choosing from the 36 flavours on offer: Mascarpone and Ricotta? Croccante (crunchy almonds, caramelized nuts, bitter chocolate and cream)? Rose d'Orient (cream, rosewater, pistachios)? Tomato and basil? Or just a cold and delicious sorbet, made with real peeled fruit, a little water and a touch of sugar?

The ices created by this Italian artisan, who in 1998 was the first in Paris to offer flower-shaped confections, are not only beautiful and original in their two-tone colours, but also excellent quality, made in the back shop every morning with no colouring or preserving agents.

If you're feeling really greedy, you can buy a litre of ice cream for €15, others will be happy with a two-flavour cornet for €3, three flavours for €4, or four flavours for €5. A fine place.

SIGHTS NEARBY

LUMIÈRE DE L'OEIL – MUSÉE DES ÉCLAIRAGES ANCIENS

4, rue Flatters 75005 Paris • Métro: Gobelins • Tel/Fax: 01 47 07 63 47
- E-mail: lumiara@aol.com • http://members.aol.com/lumiara/
- Open Tuesday to Friday 14.00–19.00 and Saturday 11.00–17.00
- Museum visits by appointment only

For over twenty-five years now, Monsieur Ara has restored and sold old lamps. Crammed into a tiny room, you'll find gas, paraffin and electric lamps, along with glass lamp chimneys, wicks, mantles, pearly fringe shades and other accessories just waiting for a buyer. In the back shop is a little museum displaying lamps run on paraffin, oil, petrol, alcohol and gas from all around the world, the oldest dating back to the 17th century. It's the only collection of its kind in France, as the proud owner will tell you. All these lamps are in working order.

CHAT BADA

23, bis rue des Écoles 75005 Paris
• Métro: Cardinal-Lemoine
• Tel: 01 43 54 27 86
• Open Monday to Saturday 11.00–19.30
• www.chat-bada.com

*A cat
to suit
everyone*

Cat lovers won't escape the claws of Chat Bada, the most monomaniacal shop in rue des Écoles. Here there is a cat to suit everyone, on a quilt cover (€155), ceramic mug (€9), chair (€25), earrings (€35), brooches (€30), T-shirt (€35), socks (€12), picture frame (€38), oven gloves (€16), magnets (€3), a tray (€20), bags (€42) …

Feline fanatics will even find a plug cover (€12), a sponge (€1,50) or a toaster (€20). The list of products on sale is as long as the cat theme is inexhaustible. But Fabienne Genevard, the shop owner and mistress of three tomcats, will tell you that when you're in love you don't count the cost. That said, the prices are very reasonable …

CAT EXCHANGE
L'ATELIER-GALERIE
218, rue Saint-Jacques 75005 Paris
• Métro: Cluny-la-Sorbonne

On the first Saturday of every month, 14.00–18.00, an afternoon is devoted to finding homes for cats at this art gallery in rue Saint-Jacques.

MARITHÉ + FRANÇOIS GIRBAUD

7, rue du Cherche-Midi 75006 Paris
- Métro: Sèvres-Babylone or Saint-Sulpice
- Tel: 01 53 63 53 63
- Open Tuesday to Saturday 10.00–19.00, Monday 11.00–19.00

Marithé and François Girbaud, avant-garde designers known throughout the world, have set up shop on the Left Bank since 2002, in a 300 m2 space on four levels, laid out on the theme of "humanature". Transparency and natural materials, like the oak furniture, predominate, while the floor is made of a grey-lilac resin.

A vertical garden

The most striking feature of the shop, however, is the vertical garden which extends from floor to floor. Installed by Patrick Blanc, a botanist and researcher at the Centre National de Recherche Scientifique (CNRS), it presents over 250 different plants.

You can find similar settings in Paris at Pershing Hall (the building's terrace, with its high vertical wall of plants, is not to be missed) as well as at the Quai Branly museum devoted to African, Asian, Oceanic and American civilizations. Also created by Patrick Blanc, the museum has the largest wall of plants in the world (800 m²).

BUY MANDRAKE ROOTS

LIBRAIRIE DE L'INCONNU
84, rue du Cherche-Midi 75006 Paris
- Métro: Duroc
- Tel: 01 42 84 82 82
- Open Monday to Saturday 9.30–19.30

The Librairie de l'Inconnu has over 5,000 reference works on esotericism: spiritualism, religion, magic, black mass, numerology & as well as a series of objects that should please fans of obscure science.

In particular you'll find the roots of the mandrake, a sturdy herbaceous plant from the Mediterranean region. It is attributed with hallucinogenic properties, but that's not all: an anti-spasmodic, anti-inflammatory and sedative medicine, healers commonly used it to ease childbirth or to counteract snake bites.

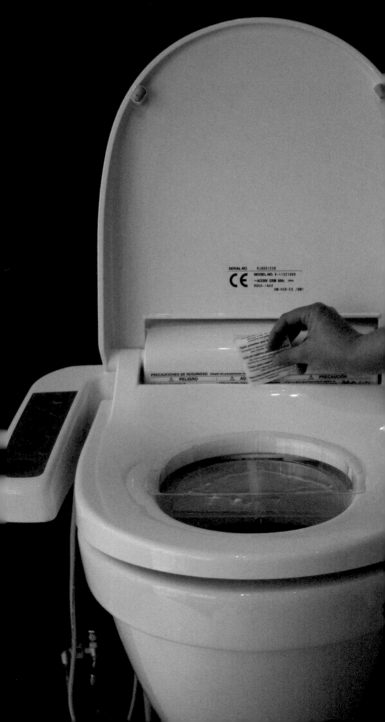

LE TRÔNE

85, rue d'Assas 75006 Paris
- Métro: Notre-Dame-des-Champs
- Tel: 01 42 45 01 73
- Open 11.00–19.00 Tuesday to Friday, and 14.00–19.00 Monday and Saturday
- www.letrone.com

*Try out
an extraordinary
Japanese WC*

Japanese WCs are coming to France. More than 50 years after the first one was sold in the land of the Rising Sun, the WC douche is on sale in this 6th arrondissement retailer. The system should go down very well with fans of all things Japanese. First you sit down on a heated seat, temperature adjustable to suit the season. When you've finished, warm water flows from a well-placed spray for a refreshing wash, thus avoiding paper waste. Ecologists will love it. In Japan, where these toilets are commonly found, people are happy to queue at the well-equipped public conveniences. Some even stay in there quite a while pampering themselves …

Finally, as at the Eléphant Bleu restaurant, comes the drying stage – with cool or warm air.

Beyond that, there are plenty more options sure to please gadget lovers: remote control, odour eaters, deodorant diffuser, water purifier and sterilizer, automatic disinfection of the spray, entry detector, automatic opening and closing. And for those who have the annoying habit of falling asleep, there is even an alarm. All this equipment is easily installed because it comes in a toilet seat that you place over the bowl. The prices begin around €900, so it's quite an investment. To convince those still hesitant about purchasing one of these intelligent seats, Le Trône has a room where you can test one out.

ATELIER RELIEUR LAMBERT BARNETT

4, rue Monsieur-le-Prince 75006
• Métro: Odéon
• Tel: 01 46 33 08 84 or 06 30 80 63 69
• Open afternoons by appointment

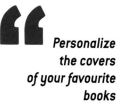

*Personalize
the covers
of your favourite
books*

Embed your child's baptism souvenir in the binding of a copy of *Little Red Riding Hood*, put a real bottle of perfume on the cover of the novel *Perfume*, insert a ring into a booklet for friends getting married, or a little statue of Buddha in *Le Bouddha Blanc* ... This is the sort of whimsy that Lambert Barnett carries out to order at his 200-year-old workshop in rue Monsieur-le-Prince.

Picture a large workspace on the ground floor of a building that formerly housed the stables and the alchemist's workshop belonging to the Prince of Condé. It's now filled with books from another age, ancient tools (including presses and a sewing machine), and one master craftsman (ex-publicist) who is deeply passionate about his work: "This is no doubt the oldest bookbinding and restoration workshop in France. We've been in the business since 1830, from father to son or daughter. That's over 200 years under the same name and in the same place!"

It goes without saying that there are plenty of memories of past achievements: "At the moment I'm restoring the grand livre des fêtes of Louis XIV. Three years ago, I bound *Le Bouddha Blanc* (winner of the Femina literary award) for the author, who wanted to include a white Buddha in the cover. And so on." More often, the artisan makes visitors' books for restaurants or special volumes ordered for retirementpresentations, for example. He is

also frequently asked by newlyweds to include wedding rings. Allow from €150 for a basic work of around 40 pages (for writing, drawing, attaching photos), for something more elaborate prices soar to €3,000. The book itself is rarely worth more than its binding, our host confides, adding: "The binding is the setting of thought". Paperbacks, mind your manner ...

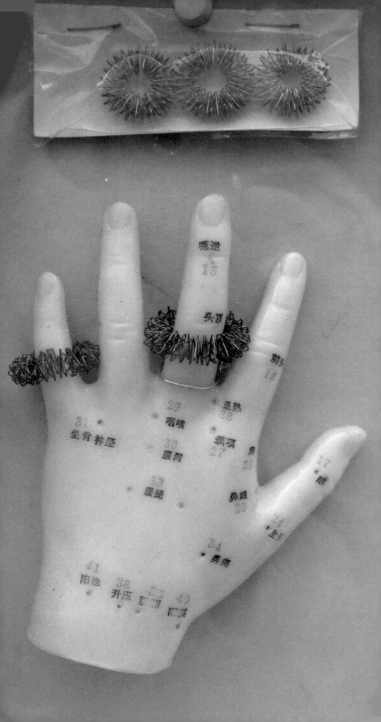

PHU-XUAN

8, rue Monsieur-le-Prince 75006 Paris
- Métro: Odéon
- Tel: 01 43 25 08 27
- Fax: 01 46 33 90 11
- Open Monday to Saturday 9.00–18.30 without interruption
- www.phuxuan.com
- E-mail: phuxuan@wanadoo.fr

> **Moxibustion, turtle lotion and magnetic patches**

Comings and goings never stop in this 6th arrondissement shop, THE temple of Asian medicine, both familiar and uncommon, in Paris. The catalogue (consultable on Internet for mail orders) is impressive: 126 pages of exotic materials and products.

Although acupuncture is obviously given pride of place, as in many such establishments, you'll also find other treatments much less well known, such as moxibustion and the placing of magnetic patches on specific parts of the body. Or you could try the turtle lotion for skin problems (€2.90).

The shop also has a library where you can find all manner of documentation on traditional Chinese medicine (note the eye yoga!).

There are even massage techniques for cats, dogs and horses. More down-to-earth are happy plasters to stick wherever it hurts. Another device that looks rather barbaric but probably very effective is a magnetic anti-wrinkle mask with patches to improve the circulation (€59). Finally, for lovers of all things Chinese, Phu Xian also sells classic slippers in black velvet (€10). The family business, originally from southern Vietnam, has been going for 25 years now. No massage, and no prescriptions, says Monsieur Phu Xuan.

MOXIBUSTION

Moxibustion treats the same points as shiatsu (acupressure) and acupuncture, the difference being that they are not pressed or pricked, but heated. Blockages are not only dissolved and the flow of energy liberated, but extra energy is brought to the body. In this way the Moxa (dried mugwort used either as a powder or in the form of a cone or a coat) is recommended as an energy booster to help with problems of cold, exhaustion and weakness.

INCOGNITO

16, rue Guénégaud 75006 Paris
- Métro: Odéon
- Tel: 01 43 25 78 38
- Open to members 24 hrs a day
- E-mail: artclub@incognito.vu

A gallery open 24/24 whose members all have a key ...

Here's an art gallery that really does trust its clients: they have the keys and can come in whenever they like, day or night. And you'd be wrong to think the place is guarded: there is no gallery owner, no sales staff, and no cameras on the premises. Just spotlights, kept turned on round the clock. Located on rue Guénégaud, at Saint-Germain-des-Prés, the place is called Incognito. The interior is like a narrow corridor. You can't miss it from the outside: its candy pink façade breaks up the harmony of this grey street. Open for three years now, Incognito is in fact a tightly knit club of lovers of contemporary art (videos, installations, photographs, paintings). In exchange for an annual fee of €500 (offset against the purchase of an artwork), the VIP members can take over the gallery, often on a flying visit as there are never more than a handful of works to look at. There are some 60 members today, all of whom have a magnetic card that lets them in at any hour.

Whose work is on display? There are a few well-known artists such as Armleder and Villéglé, but also emerging talents like Soulerin and Grancher. So, if you see a shady-looking character lurking inside this gallery late at night, don't call the police. It's just an insomniac collector …

SIGHTS NEARBY

A SPECTACULAR *HÔTEL PARTICULIER*
BONPOINT
6, rue de Tournon 75006 Paris
- Métro: Odéon • Tel: 01 40 51 98 20
- Open Monday to Saturday 10.00-19.00

The famous children's clothing label Bonpoint set up shop in February 2006 in this magnificent private mansion with 1,000 m² of floor space. It's worth a detour just to admire the architecture and interior design. If you can afford it, shopping here is also very pleasant. There's a charming tearoom and restaurant in the superb inner garden covering 600 m².

LA PISCINE

17, rue de Sèvres 75006 Paris
• Métro: Sèvres-Babylone
• Open Monday to Saturday 11.00–19.30
• Tel: 01 42 22 65 52
• www.lapiscine.fr

The former Lutetia pool is now a clothing store

From the street (rue de Sèvres) there is nothing that announces to the passer-by what awaits inside. The eponymous La Piscine is now installed in the former swimming pool of the celebrated Lutetia luxury hotel.

The visual shock is rather impressive: inside the shop, which deals only in dégriffé* designer clothing, there is a direct view of the immense Art Deco pool (now empty but for some boxes of stock lying around). The present owner has nevertheless had the (good?) taste to cover a part of the pool with fine sand and provide a few deckchairs … Unfortunately you can't get near them, a pity since they could provide an attractive place to take a rest from shopping in the neighbourhood. It's also a pity that the general atmosphere of the place is more reminiscent of Barbès than Sèvres-Babylone …

Perhaps not for much longer, however, because a place like this is obviously not lacking in prospective acquirers. Unluckily for developers, but luckily for local residents, the site is listed and the mayor of the 6th arrondissement has been trying for years to convince Bertrand Delanoë [mayor of Paris] to reopen the pool, closed now for over 30 years. The police decided

that public safety requirements were not being met: the number of exits was insufficient should there be a problem. In fact, during these last 30 years various companies have come and gone in this magnificent space - stores selling garments, decorative objects, mattresses – just about everything has passed between its venerable walls.

Today, the 6th arrondissement, together with the neighbouring 7th, has only one public swimming pool (piscine Mabillon) available to the many residents of this densely populated area. A feasibility study is underway …

*Clothing sold at a reduced price with the labels removed.

PINCELOUP

53, quai des Grands-Augustins 75006 Paris
• Métro: Saint-Michel, Odéon or Pont-Neuf
• Tel: 01 44 41 14 74
• Open Monday 12.00–19.30, Tuesday to Saturday 10.00–19.30
• www.pinceloup.fr
• E-mail: contact@pinceloup.fr

Give your dog a treat: offer it a massage

Lovers of dogs and other four-legged friends now have a theme store in the heart of the city since December 2004. Located by the river on the Left Bank between the second-hand bookstalls and antique sellers, Pinceloup occupies a bright, elegant space created by the stylist Couli Jobert and her designer daughter, Coline Roy-Camille.

The shop's originality can be summed up in three words: massages for dogs. Magali Thérouin, a therapeutic masseuse with qualifications from the Ojai School of Massage in California (!) thus offers (Mondays by appointment) "a holistic approach for the physical and emotional well-being" of your dog, your cat, or even your rabbit …

With her magical touch, Magali will relax your animal if it's nervous or give it energy and suppleness if it's tired. This rejuvenating treatment won't cost you less than €35 for 20 minutes and up to €90 for 60 minutes of massage with essential oils. As in psychiatry, a session every week is recommended …

UNICORN HORN FROM THE CHEMIST'S

PHARMACIE COTINAT

151, rue de Grenelle 75007 Paris
• Tel: 01 47 05 48 65
• Métro: Ecole Militaire
• Open 14.00–20.00 Monday, 8.30–13.00 and 14.00–20.00 Tuesday to Friday, 9.30–13.00 and 14.30–19.30 Saturday.

If you've never seen a unicorn horn up close, apart from the famous Lady and the Unicorn tapestry at the Cluny Museum (Musée National du Moyen Âge, Paris), better pop along to rue de Grenelle: the window of the local pharmacy displays what is purportedly the horn of this fabled beast. More mundanely, the object is nothing more than the tusk of a narwhal (toothed whale), a Arctic-dwelling cetacean measuring up to 4 m in length. The "tooth" on its upper jaw can grow to 3 m, which really seems rather out of proportion to the total size of the creature and may help to explain one possible origin of the legend.

EDITIONS DE PARFUMS – FRÉDÉRIC MALLE

37, rue de Grenelle 75007 Paris
- Métro: Rue-du-Bac, Saint-Sulpice
- Tel: 01 42 22 77 22
- Open Monday 13.00–19.00 and Tuesday to Saturday 11.00–19.00
- www.editionsdeparfums.com
- Other Malle shops:
  140, avenue Victor-Hugo 75116 Paris – Tel: 01 45 05 39 02
  21, rue du Mont-Thabor 75001 Paris – Tel: 01 42 22 74 10

*Columns
of perfume*

Chez Frédéric Malle, choosing the perfume that best suits your skin from among the 15 unique fragrances with sweetly evocative names is a fine art.

In his first shop, opened six years ago in the heart of Saint-Germain-des-Prés, next to the paper wedding dresses of Etienne Brunel and opposite the Michel Perry footwear shop, the young perfume designer Frédéric Malle welcomes you into a pretty uncluttered setting, but with books, furniture and personal artworks, as if it were his home.

After a few questions from the salesgirl, who tries to discover what's likely to appeal to you, your jaw will drop when it comes to smelling the perfumes: the samples are in little glass cases that diffuse the fragrance from below. By opening a window, you can inhale all the emanations … Thanks to this ingenious concept you capture perfectly the scent you'd leave in your wake if wearing each one.

"Angéliques sous la pluie", "En passant", "Lipstick Rose" or the latest creation "Carnal Flower" will in this way seduce those looking for a different and personalized fragrance created by a luxury craftsman.

Each is priced according to the cost of the main ingredients and the strength: around €120 for 100 ml and around €80 for 50 ml.

ANIMAL PORTRAITS-PHOTOS
STUDIO STAR TWO TWO – PATRICK JULLIEN
- Tel: 06 03 03 20 07
- www.patrickjullien.com

Patrick Jullien photographs your animals in amusing ways against kitsch and rococo backdrops.

DEYROLLE

46, rue du Bac 75007 Paris
• Métro: Rue-du-Bac
• Tel: 01 42 22 30 07
• Open Monday 10.00–13.00 and 14.00–19.00 and Tuesday to Saturday
  10.00–19.00
• E-mail: deyrolle@wanadoo.fr

*A veritable
natural history
museum*

Go into number 46 rue du Bac and have a quick look at the garden products on the ground floor (Le Prince Jardinier store recently took over the venerable building), forget the rather icy welcome and quickly go on up to the first floor …
Welcome to Deyrolle, the most incredible, oldest and most prestigious taxidermist* in Paris! A veritable museum, more like a curiosity shop than a retailer, Deyrolle is in fact the last Parisian taxidermist and one of the very few remaining in France. Housed since 1888 in a beautiful private mansion in the 7th arrondissement, the house of Deyrolle was founded in 1831 by natural history enthusiast Jean-Baptiste Deyrolle. His first and principal client was the state: the colour plates and stuffed animals brought in to liven up natural history lecture rooms came from his workshop.

Today a real collectors' paradise, Deyrolle has an impressive collection of stuffed animals on show (lions, elephants, zebras …), as well as superb displays of insects, butterflies, fossils and minerals. For those who like that sort of thing there are also his famous educational plates, both original and republished. Although stuffed animals from all over the world can be hired or bought, it's not cheap: a white rabbit costs €400, the immense Canadian moose €13,000, a magnificent ornamental pheasant or a South American coypu €480, and the famous tiger €30,000. Those on a tight budget can fall back on a pretty butterfly (from €5 to €300 depending on rarity) or an oddly-shaped beetle. You can even have your pet stuffed: only protected species are not accepted.

A final piece of advice: if you have any questions, just ask Yves, the kindly dyed-in-the-wool salesman who has run the place for last16 years.

---

* Taxidermy: the art of preparing (stuffing) dead animals to preserve them with a lifelike appearance. From the Greek taxis (arrangement, order) and derma (skin).

CHAPELLE NOTRE-DAME DE LA MÉDAILLE MIRACULEUSE

140, rue du Bac 75007 Paris
- Tel: 01 49 54 78 88
- Métro: Sèvres-Babylone

*Buy
a miracle
medal*

This unusual shop is clearly not like others. Sister Marie Madeleine adds the following comment: "Don't say that we sell the medals, that's not exactly the case. This isn't a shop: people simply deposit their money and the sisters [behind the counter] are only there to give change to those who don't have the right amount."

To be sure, but you do get a choice: the medal is available in several sizes, colours and materials. From €1.25 each to €12 for a set. "We don't make any profit from them, and we don't need publicity!", she assures us. Considering the throng of believers milling about in this spartanly decorated little place, you're inclined to believe her. The medals sell like hot cakes: "2 million a year!"

Once you've received yours, don't forget to have it blessed. This can be done in the nearby chapel. Several sisters work there full time during opening hours.

What's so miraculous about the medal? In November 1830, the Virgin Mary appeared to Catherine Labouré in this chapel. This vision became the focus of strong popular devotion: the Virgin requested that the now-famous medal should be struck and it has since found its way around the world. In 2005 the chapel celebrated its jubilee. Now more than 3,000 people visit the sanctuary every day, welcomed by the members of the Filles de la Charité (180 of whom, of 27 different nationalities, live in the adjacent monastery). For a statue of the Virgin as she appeared to Catherine Labouré, that is, pregnant, see the Secret Provence guidebook from this series.

BUY YOUR VERY OWN FRENCH PRESIDENT
LA LIBRAIRIE DE LA DOCUMENTATION FRANÇAISE
29, quai Voltaire 75007 Paris
- Métro: Assemblée-Nationale
- Open Monday to Friday 9.00–18.00

The Documentation Française bookstore sells official portraits of the French Heads of State. For €8 you can walk away with a poster of Pompidou, Giscard, Mitterrand, Chirac, or Sarkozy. General de Gaulle is a bargain at only €6. Perhaps that's because his large pin-ups has already broken even ...

LES ROBES EN PAPIER DE MIREILLE ETIENNE-BRUNEL

37, rue de Grenelle 75007 Paris
• Métro: Rue du Bac
• Tel: 01 45 48 26 13
• Fax: 01 45 44 64 40
• www.etienne-brunel.com

La Maison Blanche
73, rue de Paris 78470 Saint-Rémy-les-Chevreuse
• Tel: 06 60 42 85 22

Wedding gowns made from paper

Installed in a former bakery in rue de Grenelle now converted into a boudoir, the astonishing Mireille Étienne Brunel has been creating magnificent paper wedding gowns since 1997.

Seeking to transform the whole business of fitting a wedding gown into an exquisite and romantic experience, the fashion designer has done her best to create an atmosphere worthy of Alice in Wonderland once the bride-to-be steps through her door. The profusion, eccentricity and sheer personality of the models on display are simply fascinating; like these light-filtering gowns, for example, that transport you into a world of poetry and plant-like purity. They are in fact composed of two layers: a "secret" gown made from tear-proof paper that serves as a support, and over that, a more evanescent "friponne" [cheeky] gown that plays with the light and transparency. Creations like these will make the occasion truly unique.

Heavy drapes conceal the fitting room, where an attentive Mireille follows you, listens to you, and scrutinizes you … before attempting to sculpt a gown in your image. The final fitting will take place in a romantic Palladian villa located in the Chevreuse valley south of Paris.

POST OFFICE AT THE EIFFEL TOWER
PREMIER ÉTAGE DE LA TOUR EIFFEL 75007 PARIS
• Métro: Bir-Hakeim
• Open 10.00–19.00

Not many Parisians know this but the smallest, highest and most romantic Post Office in the city is perched on the first storey of the Eiffel Tower. Thinking that to send letters cancelled "Paris Tour Eiffel" is the very height of chic, some people have gone so far as to post their wedding invitations from up there. You can now send faxes, too, just to show off!

This is also the only Post Office with an entry fee: €4.10 for an adult as far as the first platform, €2.30 for children 3 to 11 years. On the first storey, you'll also find an exhibition space, an observatory for viewing activity at the top of the tower, and the Féeroscope (to find out how the monument was built), among other attractions.

MICHEL CHAUDUN

149, rue de l'Université 75007 Paris
• Métro: La Tour-Maubourg
• Tel: 01 47 53 74 40
• Open 9.15–19.00 Tuesday to Saturday, 10.00–18.00 Monday

*Offer
a chocolate ring,
hedgehog
or horse*

This shop should be made part of the public health service. You'll find the best chocolate here in all shapes and sizes, even the most unlikely. Michel Chaudun, artisan and celebrity in his field, makes rings (€2.10) and bracelets, Eiffel towers, snails, hedgehogs, even Yorkshire terriers and poodles (around €9 for a small figure in dark, white or milk chocolate)! Much more spectacular are his giant Easter eggs, his Hermès bags, and his realistic horse sculptures, all made entirely from chocolate.

His shop is a treasure-trove paying tribute to this irresistible substance, which is home-made (in fact, a mixture of three types prepared to a secret recipe). Chaudun is his own best customer: he admits to devouring at least one bar every evening and never travels without a stock. When he runs out of chocolate on one of his trips, he is capable of making a 60 km detour to find some. All this gives him the energy to fly round the world several times a year to sell his products in Tokyo, where he already has two shops.

With those who equate chocolate with liver damage, he takes umbrage: there can be no criticism of his consuming passion in this shop. Although it may dismay gourmands feeling guilt, the insatiable shop owner has remained quite slender. But he does admit that for him, "It's impossible to start a bar without finishing it. It takes great willpower not to help myself to another. And if you have a whole box, don't ever pass it to me …"

CHOCOLATE BOUQUETS!
LE FLEURISTE DU CHOCOLAT
49, avenue de la Bourdonnais 75007 Paris • Métro École-Militaire
• Open Monday to Saturday 9.30–19.00 • www.lefleuristeduchocolat.com
The *pâtissier-chocolatier* Thierry Bonnet has had the clever idea of producing edible bouquets. They are made from chocolate as well as brown sugar, sugared almonds or marshmallow. The lucky recipient of the bouquet is bound to melt with pleasure.

OTHER CHOCOLATE SCULPTURES
CHOCOLATS ROCHOUX 16, rue d'Assas 75006 Paris • Tel: 01 42 84 29 45

LA GRANDE HERBORISTERIE

31, rue d'Amsterdam 75008 Paris
- Métro: Liège or Place-de-Clichy
- Tel: 01 48 74 83 32
- Open Monday 11.00-13.00 and 14.00-19.00, Tuesday to Friday
  10.00–13.00 and 14.00–19.00 and Saturday 10.00-13.00 and 14.00-18.00

The finest herbalist in Paris

The interior of this shop alone is worth a visit. Not only because of the oak wood-work, infinitely elegant though it is (there are others like it in Paris), but because of the collection of white packets and flask with rather mysterious contents on the shelves. At the back of shop is the apo-thecary's laboratory: a man in a white coat shakes and mixes powders, herbs, and liquids, preparing potions like some mad professor absorbed by his pains-taking formulas. Although the atmosphere is fascinating (a change from clini-cal modern pharmacies), the herbalist's shop at place de Clichy is of particular interest for the treatments it offers based on purely natural products. Coughs, menopause, insomnia, depression, stress, cold sores … the list is long: 80% of these kinds of problems can be remedied.

This establishment has specialized in medicinal plants since 1880. Although there used to be as many herbalists as pharmacists, the profession went into decline after 1941 when the herbalist's diploma was abolished. The extremely well-preserved shop was given a new lease of life when Jean-Pierre Raveneau took over 13 years ago. "I was walking past and fell in love with the place. As it happened it was for sale, so I bought it …" This dedicated herbalist accurately foresaw the comeback of alternative medicine "since 1996, when the pharma-ceutical laboratories were obliged to mention the possible side-effects of their medication …"

Among the 900 types of plants available, including hibiscus (refreshing) and water lily (sexual depressant, not in great demand!), are some really exotic ones. For example, the mystical pepper from the Fiji islands which apparently works as a tranquilliser. Or the Burmese lichen with beneficial effects in organ trans-plants.

THE BLACK LIFT OF MAGASIN LOUIS VUITTON

101, avenue des Champs-Élysées 75008 Paris
• Métro: Georges-V
• Tel: 01 53 57 52 00
• Open Monday to Saturday 10.00–20.00,
  Sunday 11.00–13.00 and 14.00–19.00

*Light
in the darkness*

The Louis Vuitton temple on the Champs-Élysées is not just an up-market store. Its superb décor, embellished with works by modern artists (including a magnificent piece by James Turrell), is well worth a look. But perhaps its most surprising feature is the lift, which is completely blacked out. It may seem strange to want to enclose your customers in pitch darkness between two floors, but there's a good reason: upon entering the lift compartment, the visitor is meant to pass into a Zen-like state. This "little room of sensory entropy" created by Olafur Eliasson is supposed to encourage people "to reflect on the ways in which they define their presence in space and consequently their consciousness of self". The lift has been lined with a material that looks like black wool and absorbs sound. Microphones pick up sounds inside and speakers relay negative sound waves, the effect of which is near total silence. There is no light emitted, not even from the lift buttons. The ride lasts 20 seconds and "won't frighten anyone", as the artist said reassuringly before the shop opened. Unfortunately, sometimes the opposite is true, as one of the sales staff told us. During the Christmas festivities the lift was shut down, because "the crowds could have started a panic". So if you're claustrophobic, you'd better stick to the escalator. Make up for it by admiring the impressive atrium with its 1,900 suspended stainless-steel rods.

You'll probably have to queue to get into the building, however, since the Vuitton products sold here are less expensive than in Asia and attract many Japanese and Chinese customers … who are rather closely watched by store security in case they're buying on behalf of clandestine workshops looking for an original to copy.

SIGHTS NEARBY

VIVRASIE: ANTIQUE FURNITURE AND RARE OBJECTS FROM ASIA

85, boulevard Malesherbes 75008 Paris • Métro: Saint-Augustin
• Tel: 01 55 30 00 06 • E-mail: aline.pintaud@vivrasie.com
• Open until 22.00, by appointment with Aline Pintaud

Located on the first floor of a building in the 8th arrondissement, Aline Pintaud's gallery has some superb pieces of Asian art and furniture. Although you need to book your visit, there are viewings and open days organized throughout the year. "For anyone too shy to make an appointment," the gallery owner stresses … The gallery does in fact extend a friendly, personalized welcome, which is precisely what attracts customers in the know to this haven while others wear themselves out dashing along boulevard Haussmann on a Saturday afternoon. Several times a year, Aline goes off on trips to Asia to renew her stock. If you place an advance order with her, she may bring you back that Buddha or gong you've been dreaming about.

216 RIVOLI – VÉRONIQUE DES ROTOURS

38, rue de Courcelles 75008 Paris
• Métro: Miromesnil
• Tel: 01 40 08 00 20
• Portable: 06 81 84 07 99
• E-mail: vdesrotours216@yahoo.fr
• www.216rivoli.com

Tailoring for all the family under one roof

Mum, Dad and the children can now be fitted out to match! Vivacious blonde designer Véronique des Rotours will take care of that. Just make an appointment at her place, where you'll find the home-made feeling that she has built around her label, 216 Rivoli, launched four years ago.

"I began making and selling made-to-measure suits in an attic studio at place de Clichy, where I had to stand the bed on end to make space for fittings! Then in two houseboats where I was living … I've even shown garments in a van parked outside fashion shows! As bohemian as could be, and the magazines, especially the Japanese ones, just loved it. I had photo spreads appearing one after the other!"

Today the 30-year-old, who trained with Nina Ricci, has left her garret to set herself up with greater seriousness, and with a partner, in a two-room apartment in the 8th arrondissement. Less fun perhaps, but still as successful as ever.

So her workshop and office are now located on the top floor of an elegant building in rue de Courcelles, which has become a meeting place for part of the Parisian smart set. There the designer presents her collection of tailored suits to ambitious working girls, style-conscious men, and fashionable rich kids. In this business district (offices everywhere), push open the heavy door, cross the courtyard and climb into the little lift that goes up to Véronique's floor. At the end of a very Seventies-style corridor, a door is open. The coffee is already made and the outfits are just waiting to be tried on. You follow the young woman into the bedroom under the eaves. This is where it all happens, between two Velux windows, next to a bed covered with a bright red fake fur, among hangers, bits of leftover cloth, patterns tacked to the wall, and magnificent fabrics recuperated from some of the big fashion houses. The suits, impeccably cut, in resolutely chic materials (damask, velvet, satin, jacquard, prints) and androgynous in style, wait their turn on tailor's dummies.

You'll want to try them on right away. Even more so as the prices are affordable: starting at €600 for a tailored suit signed 216 Rivoli. There's a story behind the young designer's label: "My grandmother lived at no. 216, rue de Rivoli, and I always dreamed of setting up shop there, it was sublime!" Indeed!

GALERIE C.T. LOO & CIE

48, rue de Courcelles 75008 Paris
- Métro: Courcelles, Saint-Philippe-du-Roule or Monceau
- Tel: 01 45 62 53 15
- Open Thursday and Saturday 14.00–18.00, other days by appointment
- E-mail: ct.loo@hotE-mail.fr

Gallery/ museum in a Chinese pagoda

In the heart of the Plaine Monceau district, alongside the traditional buildings from the Haussmann period, stands an incredible Chinese pagoda.
Designed in 1926 by French architect Fernand Bloch for the Chinese antique dealer, Ching-Tsai Loo, on the site of a former Louis-Philippe mansion, C.T. Loo & Cie is still the oldest Asian art gallery in Paris, and the city's only authentic Chinese building. With over 600 m2 on six floors, it offers a unique architectural framework and particularly refined interiors: an original moon door, Chinese 17th- and 18th-century lacquered woodwork, a ceiling made of Art Deco glass slabs, a superb Indian gallery in 18th- and 19-century carved wood, a lift covered in lacquered wood, and a delightful Zen-like atmosphere marked by the passage of time …

In this unique place, you'll come across French people and foreigners (many Americans), collectors and families, as well as interior designers interested in the modern lacquered furniture made by the gallery. Among the items for sale are a 19th-century Chinese elm wood bench at €1,500, a superb 18th-century silk painting showing ladies of the court at €5,500,

archaeological artefacts in ancient earthenware from the Han and Wei dynasties, or a pair of armchairs in hongmu (a type of Chinese mahogany) dating from the 18th century, €18,000.

Those on a budget will also find something pleasing among the delicate Chinese prints from the 18th and 19th centuries at €180 and €120 each, or modern objects such as a vase made from lacquered eggshells at €100.

Certain rooms of the gallery can be hired for cocktails, press conferences, fashion shows or receptions …

LA NOUVELLE ATHÈNES

1, rue de Liège 75009 Paris – left, 2nd floor
- Métro: Liège, Saint-Lazare or Place-de-Clichy
- Tel: 01 48 74 86 89
- Open Tuesday, Thursday, Friday and Saturday from 10.00 (last haircut 18.00)
- E-mail: contact@sylviecoudray.com
- From €60 per cut

Home hairdressing

Have your hair done as if you were at a friend's place, in glamorous yet cosy and intimate surroundings. In the heart of the 9th arrondissement, La Nouvelle Athènes invites you into its magnificent apartment dating from the Haussmann period: mouldings, parquet, red velvet curtains, Art Deco wooden furniture and works of art on the walls, it's all there. Outside there's no sign, you have to know about it. On the second floor, you're soon seduced by the atmosphere: with a delicious cup of tea in your hand and Aretha Franklin playing quietly in the background, you'll see Oliver the cat curled up on the cushioned sofas …

Sylvie Coudray opened this discreet and original place in September 2004. A trained plastic surgeon, and a devotee of second-hand stalls and Art Deco, her only rule is to "make people beautiful". Here trends are forgotten and a personalized hair treatment is provided.

Sébastien or Isabelle, the two hairdressers trained by Sylvie, consider the clients' profile, advise them, talk about their hair almost as if it were a work of art, and finally dry-cut it.

You'll find just as many local women from the neighbourhood who come every week for their shampoo and set as you will trendsetting bobos [bourgeois-bohème], or even provincial ladies treating themselves after a shopping expedition in the nearby department stores. Men are also beginning to try out the place. The best thing is that nobody will notice you've just come from the hairdresser: here the natural look comes first. The only disadvantage is that the salon chairs are rather hard and don't really let you get comfortable.

Prices range from €60 for a haircut to between €75 and €100 for a full colour treatment by Mélanie the magician and €120 for a proper hairdressing lesson, which will show you how to manage the style yourself following a set of personalized photos retracing the various steps. Note that its great success means that La Nouvelle Athènes is planning to move to larger premises, but we're told that the "home sweet home" spirit will still be there.

LA MAISON JARDIN

24 rue Choron 75009 Paris
• Métro: Notre-Dame-de-Lorette
• Tel: 01 42 81 35 59
• Open Tuesday to Sunday 9.00–20.00

Bouquets of weeds

There are florists and florists. Not only is this one particularly charming, but also a certain originality is guaranteed. Lovers of wild flowers or even "pretty" weeds take note that La Maison Jardin puts together its sublime bouquets from "practically nothing".

The shop, at the beginning of rue des Martyrs, is hidden behind a huge display of flowers and plants. The inside is the same: narrow but invaded by nature in all its glory, just like the atypical but welcoming florist, her face as radiant as a bunch of sunflowers.

"If I had to define my style? Between the vicarage and the English cottage garden," says Corinne, who set up her business ten years ago in this former upholsterer's workshop. Poppies, daisies, roses and budding branches are reflected in the many mirrors around the shop while paper butterflies flit across the ceiling. Corinne doesn't hesitate to go out and pick flowers from the fields and hedgerows. She also deals in second-hand goods: every stick of furniture in the shop is for sale. A good time to visit is on Sunday, during "Happy Flower": "I clear the shop then, so to get rid of the stock I sell all the flowers by the bucketful."

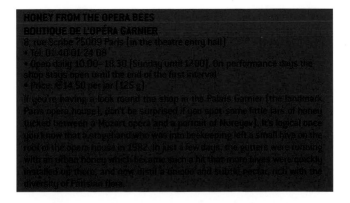

HONEY FROM THE OPERA BEES
BOUTIQUE DE L'OPÉRA GARNIER
8, rue Scribe 75009 Paris (in the theatre entry hall)
• Tel: 01 40 01 24 08
• Open daily 10.00–18.30 (Sunday until 17.00). On performance days the shop stays open until the end of the first interval
• Price: € 14.50 per jar (125 g)

If you're having a look round the shop in the Palais Garnier (the landmark Paris opera house), don't be surprised if you spot some little jars of honey tucked between a Mozart opera and a portrait of Nureyev. It's logical once you know that a stagehand who was into beekeeping left a small hive on the roof of the opera house in 1982. In just a few days, the gutters were running with an urban honey which became such a hit that more hives were quickly installed up there, and now distil a unique and subtle nectar, rich with the diversity of Parisian flora.

Detaille
1905
PARIS

DETAILLE

10, rue Saint-Lazare 75009 Paris
• Métro: Saint-Lazare
• Tel: 01 48 78 68 50
• Open Monday 15.00–19.00, Tuesday to Saturday 10.00–13.30 and 14.00–19.00
• www.detaille.com

Anti-pollution balm

Seen from the street, the little shop Detaille (pronounced Deu-taille), next to the Saint-Lazare train station, doesn't look like anything special. Inside, however, you'll discover the unusual "Automobile" balm invented by the Countess of Presle, an early 20th-century grande bourgeoise.

At the time, having acquired one of the early motor vehicles, the countess felt that her skin was drying out because of the unaccustomed speed, not to mention the lack of a windscreen. She mentioned this to a friend, chemist Marcellin Berthelot, who created a hydrating balm to protect the face during the day. So pollution is nothing new. This "non-greasy liquid with protective qualities" contains zinc oxide, other minerals and wheat protein.

Thus was born the original Automobile formula. In 1905, the house of Detaille, named after the countess's husband, was launched. And almost a hundred years later, the shop, elegantly decorated with period pieces, is still selling its illustrious balm. Although the formula has been modified slightly to respect current regulations, the shop has kept its faithful customers from mother to daughter.

From these premises, which have only changed hands three times since the

Detaille family sold up, the treasured products have been exported to all the courts of Europe. "The names of the Queen of Bulgaria, the Queen of Belgium, several maharajahs, countesses, and princesses … fill its visitors' books."

Automobile balm costs €39 for 60 ml (€65 for 125 ml, €116 for 250 ml).

Other products are available: toilet water with names as subtle as Aeroplane, candles, creams, lotions, and hair oils. In addition to Automobile balm, we recommend Fleur de riz face powder. Its three corrective tints have been made according to the same formula since 1900. As the name indicates, it is actually powdered rice.

AURA PHOTO

58, rue du Faubourg Montmartre 75009 Paris
- Métro: Le Peletier, Notre-Dame-de-Lorette or Grands-Boulevards
- Tel: 01 41 71 19 44 and 01 48 78 64 10
- With or without appointment from Tuesday to Saturday
- www.aura-photo.fr

*Snap
your aura*

Their advertisements might make you smile. Yet once inside the shop you want to believe them. As the name certainly indicates, Aura Photo offers to take pictures of your aura.

The dictionary definition of an aura is "a supposed emanation surrounding the body of a living creature, visible only to initiate." Indeed, this is the case here, although the initiate in question is in fact a "Spectrometer" camera.

Welcomed by Madame Danièle Laurent, a qualified practitioner trained in the United States and moreover a charming person, you sit down in her studio after a brief chat about the method. You place each hand on metal plates linked to the camera. Smile and it's in the box. In the time it takes the Polaroid to dry, your aura is imprinted on paper.

Other than its undeniable aesthetic qualities (some artists have used the same procedure), the photo can be very revealing. Depending on the colours, the size and the intensity of the halo produced by the aura, Madame Laurent can analyse your personality and give you some lifestyle advice (the session of around an hour costs €30 with photo).

There is in any case no shortage of customers. A mother even came along with her two babies for a "halo-cinatory" family portrait!

AURA

An aura is a coloured glow supposedly emanating from the surface of an object; not to be confused with the halos of saints, which in Christian iconography are used to represent divine radiance. It is thought to be the manifestation of an electromagnetic field or the vital energy in all things.

Normally, auras are only visible to those gifted with psychic powers. However, with a little training, or thanks to aura glasses fitted with a special filter (found in any good New Age boutique), anyone can see them.

The Kirlian contact process (named after a 1950s Soviet researcher), also makes it possible to "photograph" auras.

PHONOGALERIE

10, rue Lallier 75009 Paris
- Métro: Anvers
- Tel/Fax: 01 45 26 45 80
- Mobile: 06 80 61 59 37
- E-mail: aro@phonogalerie.com
- www.phonogalerie.com
- Open Monday to Saturday 10.00–13.00 and 14.00–19.00
- Guided tours without booking for groups of three to four, larger groups should book

A collection of talking machines

Jalal Aro is more than just a collector: he treats, heals and restores life to any object relating to sound recordings. After several years spent collecting the most astonishing talking machines since their invention in 1877 (cylindrical devices, gramophones with horns, music boxes), he finally opened up a store devoted to sound. There you'll find advertising posters, musical postcards and old records, as well as some unusual and sophisticated machines; although in the interest of maintaining certain aesthetic standards, objects from the last thirty years are banned. The owner will surely help you choose a gift (prices range from €5 to €15,000), but above all, enthuse you with his anecdotes and deep knowledge of his subject.

LE FURET TANRADE

63, rue de Chabrol 75010 Paris
• Métro: Poissonnière
• Tel: 01 47 70 48 34
• Open Monday to Saturday 8.00–19.45, Sunday 9.00–19.00

Beaujolais nouveau jelly to celebrate the wine harvest, chocolate with hemp, and pumpkin jam for Halloween … Le Furet Tanrade is just the place if you're tired of the same old thing. These confectioners specializing in jams, chocolate and tea have been in business since 1728. In their new shop in rue de Chabrol (formerly in rue Vignon), respect for tradition is everything: the fruit has been picked in the same place for 55 years and old-fashioned recipes are always used.

> *Beaujolais jelly, or jam with sweet pepper, courgette, walnut and cinnamon*

The present confectioner Alain Le Furet took over from the Tanrade family in 1990, having worked in the Lenôtre and Boissier kitchens. His most unusual jam? The one with sweet pepper, courgette, walnut and cinnamon. All jars are €5.

DES HABITS ET VOUS

22, rue Jean-Moinon 75010 Paris
- Métro: Belleville or Colonel-Fabien
- Tel: 01 40 18 91 66
- Open by appointment

*A stylist
who uses
only remnants*

An endearing little shop in an equally charming street, Des Habits et Vous makes and sells garments, fashion accessories and rugs (ranging in price from €5 to €300, around €100 for a skirt) in a perfectly chaotic setting. Its speciality is to recycle scraps from the textile industry by transforming them. A great idea. The designer, Dani Michels, whom we met one rainy December day when she returned from a trip to Senegal, explains:

"Every day in Paris, tons of fabric off-cuts are thrown out by the textile workshops. As the rubbish isn't sorted separately, vast quantities of fabric are incinerated with the domestic waste. By salvaging and fashioning these small pieces of fabric (which then become my source material) into an economically viable product, I'm showing that from our rubbish we can create riches.

So far I've set up an association that provides work for two people who were having great difficulties integrating themselves into society. The profits have been used to carry out a project in Mali. I'm now working on another in Madagascar."

You must go there and see for yourselves. Dani Michels designs pretty ethno-chic garments in very good taste.

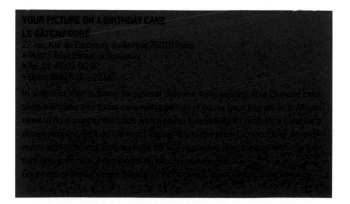

YOUR PICTURE ON A BIRTHDAY CAKE
LE GÂTEAU DORÉ

AUDE et PHILIPPE

LA FLEUR

et

E PAPILLO

TOILETTES
USAGE LIMITE
A 5 mn

ENTREPRISE JACQUIN

18, boulevard des Filles-du-Calvaire 75011 Paris
- Tel: 01 47 00 50 95
- Open Monday to Friday 9.00–13.00 and 14.00–18.00
- Métro: Filles-du-Calvaire

"

*Have
a plaque
engraved
with your name*

Street names, house numbers, dange-rous dog, friendly dog, no entry, bewa-re traps, private fishing, emergency exit, research centre, infirmary, etc. The workshop of Entreprise Jacquin not only has an impressive quantity of ready-made plates, but also engraves all sorts of messages, addresses, and so forth, to order.

Allow 15 days for a simple engraving, and between four and five weeks for an enamelled plaque. Their bestselling line? For an anniversary or retirement, the workshop will engrave the name of the person, together with Place or Avenue, on a plate like those you see on the streets of Paris.

For only €8 you can buy small plaques with captions such as Chien lunatique, Chat perché, Chien cool, etc.

STREET FURNITURE FOR HIRE
RÉGIFILM
60, rue Amelot 75011 Paris
- Métro: Chemin-Vert or Saint-Sébastien-Froissart
- Tel: 01 43 55 52 55
- Open Monday to Friday 9.00–12.30 and 14.00–18.00
- www.regifilm.com

This place near the Bastille hires out costumes (an impressive collection of outfits, civilian and military, representing history from antiquity to the present, from Nefertiti to the last Emperor of China) and other accessories to individuals, theatres, film makers or television.

Unlike rival costume hirers, Régifilm also offers a wide choice of ancient or modern street furniture (public benches, gas lamps, traffic lights, newspaper kiosks, Morris columns).

CYBERPIANO

6, rue Sedaine 75011 Paris
• Métro: Bastille or Bréguet-Sabin
• Tel: 01 47 00 92 47
• Open Tuesday to Friday 11.00–22.00, Saturday and Sunday 11.00–20.00
• www.cyber-piano.fr

*No space
for a piano
at home ...?*

All kinds of people visit Cyberpiano: those with little spare cash, musicians on tour, piano students, curious passers-by … Managed along the similar lines to an internet café, the principle is simple and a great idea: twelve pianos are available (€1 for 10 minutes, 20% reduction for students), in a room that manages to be both neutral and convivial. The ambiance is calm and the proprietor, Michel, himself a pianist in his spare time, is very likeable.

Passing pianists can work either wearing headphones or in one of the two cabins located in the basement. The equipment is new (the place opened in June 2005) and of good quality. There is a traditional upright piano, several digital uprights "with very realistic feel and sound" and two concert pianos. Michel gives lessons (€30 an hour) and makes good coffee (€1.50).

Finally, for those who might be asking why "cyber", the programme is interactive because anyone can record on a CD (from the keyboard or by voice recording in the cabins), and head for the recording studio with a faultless demonstration disc!

DOCTEUR GUILLAUME – LA CLINIQUE DU RASOIR
42, rue de la Roquette 75011 Paris
• Métro: Bastille
• Tel: 01 47 00 12 70
• Open 10.30–12.30 and 16.00–19.30 Monday to Saturday

Your electric razor isn't feeling well. It doesn't get to the root of the problem like it used to. Don't panic just go along to Doctor Guillaume's razor clinic. Since the 1950s, Jacques Guillaume has been repairing faulty machines. It is even said that he repaired President Mitterrand's razors. His shop is barely 5 m², and you have to squeeze in between the clutter of spare parts and the owner's scooter, which is also parked in there.

CONSOLE

14, rue de la Folie-Régnault 75011 Paris
- Métro: Philippe-Auguste or Charonne
- Tel: 01 43 56 28 22
- Ground floor, rear of courtyard
- Open by appointment or consult website
- E-mail: c.o.n.s.o.l.e@free.fr
- http://c.o.n.s.o.l.e.free.fr/

A distinctive showcase for modern art

At first glance, there's nothing to distinguish this apartment-cum-workshop in the 11th arrondissement from any of the numerous other industrial buildings that have been transformed into residential accommodation by Parisians wanting a different lifestyle. Muriel Colin-Barrand and Pierre Lardeau live in this creative space where the remains of the former foundry are still clearly visible: an imposing industrial chimney in brick, bare concrete, a skylight, and the factory roof … These two "young forty-somethings" extend a simple but warm welcome to passing visitors. Are they the last defenders of the forgotten tradition of hospitality? Not exactly …

Console, an apartment-gallery and experimental space since 2001, is an entire concept that offers painters, sculptors,, writers, designers and musicians a chance to work together and make full use of its 220 m². Madame, a dynamic independent exhibition curator who is currently working for the Musée du Quai Branly, and Monsieur, a versatile artist, fervently and passionately animate this venue, unique in the contemporary art world. Ranging from a drawing board with movable shelf to a low zinc table, the pieces produced by Pierre Lardeau will cost you between €300 and €2,000.

There is a permanent display of works for sale (a wall drawing by François-Xavier Courrèges, a rat frieze by Arnika Müll, a sound installation by Emmanuel Lagarrigue, thousands of hematite crystals embedded in the bare concrete wall by Amande In …), but the space is flexible and can be reconfigured for temporary exhibitions. In the pretty corner equipped for reading or listening to recordings, you'll find a small shop selling CDs, videos, books and designer T-shirts. Finally, Console offers "AG glo" weekends (concerts with aperitif, artists' video shows and short films, showcasing electronic music, sale of recordings from independent labels, lectures, performances …).

ARÔM

73, avenue Ledru-Rollin 75012 Paris
• Métro: Ledru-Rollin
• Tel: 01 43 46 82 59
• Open Tuesday to Saturday 10.00—20.00

Black Christmas trees

Not only is the setting original and the plants bizarre, but this friendly florist likes nothing better than to choose the flowers in your bouquet himself. Just describe who they are intended for and Saber, or his associate Fabien, will do the rest.

In an anarchic setting, among pots of flowers, moss on the ceiling, African artefacts, and grasses galore, these two iconoclasts, an engineer and a sociologist, create floral compositions according to their inspiration. The shop's cluttered look, resembling that of a workshop, is of course intentional: "people really like that". It makes them feel relaxed.

Similarly, there is no limit to how little you can spend: "With just one flo-

wer, you can make a very pretty bouquet. In this neighbourhood there are plenty of people who haven't the means to spend even ?40 on flowers, and who come in with a handful of coins. Even they usually go away very pleased," says Saber.

To make the local trendies sit up and take notice, they don't hesitate to use brambles or to blacken their Christmas trees. Their creations have a dark, baroque streak, and are a far cry from French classical gardens ...

PLANÈTE DÉTECTION

22, rue Charles-Baudelaire 75012 Paris
- Métro: Ledru-Rollin
- Tel: 01 43 07 55 02
- Open 10.30–19.00 Monday to Friday
- www.planetedetection.com

Treasure hunting

Welcome to the specialist treasure hunter. Established for some years a few hundred metres from place d'Aligre, Planète Détection sells metal detectors to those who dream of one day discovering their grandparents' hidden treasure in the garden. There's a model to suit everyone, large or small. The basic one, not very expensive (around €150) is easy to use and perfectly suitable for adolescents just nosing around. "We also sell a lot as retirement presents," adds the salesman. Over and above the impressive collection of metal detectors in the window (there are also second-hand models), the shop is run by two professional treasure-hunters, experienced in unusual finds and the authors of several books on the subject. They travel all over France, detectors in hand, to dig out ingots hidden in people's cellars, or a jar of sovereigns buried in the garden, whose owner had forgotten where he hid it.

And finders keepers: the hunters of Planète Détection claim to score 20 valuable finds per year. They are most often rewarded in kind, as allowed by law: 50% of a treasure goes to the finder, the other half to the owner of the land. The salesman confides that many French people still hide their pot of gold in a corner of the vegetable patch, well away from the taxman. The treasure hunt seems to have a bright future in store for itself …

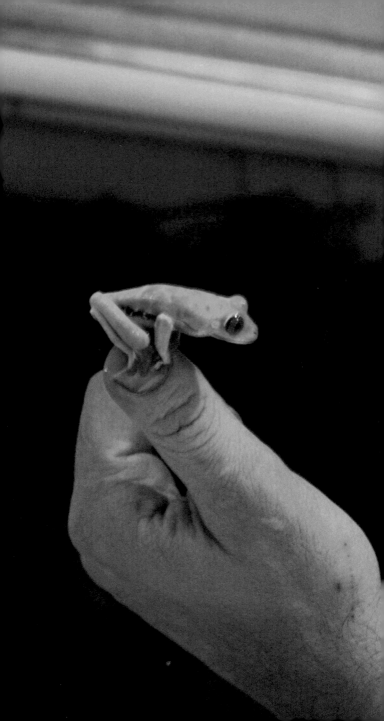

LA FERME TROPICALE

54, rue Jenner 75013 Paris
• Métro: Nationale
• Tel: 01 45 84 24 36
• Open Monday to Saturday 10.00—13.00 and 14.00—19.00
• www.lafermetropicale.com

The biggest reptile house in Europe

Can you resist this charming little exotic beast? Unless you know its Latin name you'd have no chance of taking it home, because to buy it you'd have to show your credentials, demonstrating your interest and familiarity with the species. La Ferme Tropicale confirms that it only sells to connoisseurs. "We aren't a garden centre. We don't hold with "fast-food" purchases! We sell animals, and moreover, they're delicate animals, so there's no question of following fashion," exclaims Teddy Moncuit, the director of this vast emporium. With over 600 m2 on two floors, it houses reptiles, amphibians and invertebrates. Established 11 years ago in the 13th arrondissement, this reptile house, the largest in Europe, keenly defends its reputation for reliability and professionalism. Consequently the list of lodgers is impressive: boas, pythons, grass snakes, tortoises, frogs and all kinds of spiders. "Non-poisonous", the proprietor specifies … That doesn't mean you won't need courage to keep your cool when confronted with all these vivaria. Iguana fans will be sure to spot the two specimens belonging to the house: they're enormous. Worst of all, however, is the shelf where the boxes of live "food" are stacked: grasshoppers, crickets, larvae, flies, cockroaches, etc. Bon appétit! Joking apart, La Ferme Tropicale is a unique place that lovers of all these beasties will adore. For those with a real phobia, the shop organizes desensitization courses upon request.

CUSTARD APPLE OR GINGER CARAMEL ICE CREAM
GLACIER LA TROPICALE
180, boulevard Vincent Auriol 75013 Paris
• Métro: Place d'Italie
• Tel: 01 42 16 87 27
• Open Monday to Friday 12.00—19.00, Saturday 12.00—20.00 and Sunday 15.00—19.00

An ice cream manufacturer who offers original flavours: lemon/blood orange, strawberry/mint leaves, "corossol" (tropical fruit with a sweet, creamy yellow, "custard-like" pulp) or even ginger/caramel and the delicious honey/pinenuts. There are around 80 to choose from. All the ices are homemade and the sorbets based on real fruit.
€2 single ice cream, €3.80 double.

PHOTO CINÉ GOBELINS

71, avenue des Gobelins 75013 Paris
• Métro: Place-d'Italie
• Tel: 01 43 31 34 15
• Open 9.30–12.00 and 14.30–19.30 Monday to Saturday

*A unique
camera shop*

Y ou can barely squeeze inside here. Even then it's one at a time: Monsieur Vu Dinh's shop is crammed to the ceiling with all kinds of cameras, lenses, films and flashes.

A tiny space remains so you can open and shut the door then wedge yourself in between Monsieur and Madame Vu Dinh, the shopkeepers. Luckily both are slender in build …

The couple, who come from Vietnam, have been here for 20 years. That's at least how long it would take to achieve this extraordinary jumble, almost a work of art. But when it's a matter of selling a camera from the middle of the heap, and pulling it out might bring down all the rest, it's another story …

Monsieur Vu Dinh, who jokingly refers to himself as an archaeologist,

explains: "Everything saleable is within reach. And expensive items are on the high shelves. I'm obsessed with theft. Here, I'm the only one who knows which cameras are valuable.

To buy something you only have to ask this courteous and chatty man, an expert in photographic equipment. He knows his stock by heart, having acquired it rummaging through second-hand stalls. The prices are good. But don't ask him to sell you a Leica M6 for €500, he's bound to reply: "I don't do miracles."

LIBRAIRIE ALIAS

21, rue Boulard 75014 Paris
- Métro: Denfert-Rochereau
- Tel: 01 43 21 29 82
- Open Tuesday to Saturday "never before 11.00, always after 20.00", Sunday 11.00–14.00 and Monday 14.00–20.00
- www.alias-art.com

Books in an extraordinary setting

Librairie Alias is a good place to know about, a bookseller to note in your address book, but not only that. It's also a very personalized place and an extraordinary setting.

First of all, should you go in there one day, try to refrain from asking the owner the recurring question, "How do you get a book out without all the rest falling down?"

The constant joking about this no longer amuses Monsieur Léobold, although otherwise he's an extremely pleasant fellow. You'll risk annoying him unnecessarily, which in this labyrinthine bookshop with hardly any shelving, and 30,000 art books arranged in vertical piles according to some incomprehensible plan, is hardly a very good idea …

So, slender readers, squeeze your way between the columns of books rising to the ceiling. As for those who can't get through, ask Monsieur Léobold, who knows exactly where everything is. And don't be surprised if he comes out of his den to rummage in his car parked just outside. It, too, is stuffed full of books.

What will you find here? Books on the arts, including all or almost all disciplines: painting, sculpture, architecture, photography and design, as well as theatre, opera, music, dance and cinema.

Alias is also just the tip of the iceberg, as for 25 years Monsieur Léobold has accumulated tens of thousands of books in various places (garages, sheds, depots). His dream would be to bring all his treasures together under the same roof, and to set up a cultural centre. Property owners note: he's still looking for a suitable place …

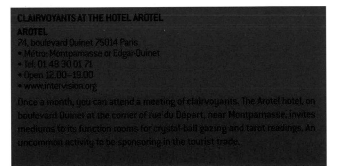

CLAIRVOYANTS AT THE HOTEL AROTEL

AROTEL
74, boulevard Quinet 75014 Paris
- Métro: Montparnasse or Edgar-Quinet
- Tel: 01 48 30 01 71
- Open 12.00–19.00
- www.intervision.org

Once a month, you can attend a meeting of clairvoyants. The Arotel hotel, on boulevard Quinet at the corner of rue du Départ, near Montparnasse, invites mediums to its function rooms for crystal-ball gazing and tarot readings. An uncommon activity to be sponsoring in the tourist trade.

PUZZLE MICHÈLE WILSON

97, avenue Émile-Zola 75015 Paris
- Métro: Charles-Michel or Émile-Zola
- Tel: 01 45 75 35 28
- Open Monday to Friday 9.00–19.00, Saturday 10.00–19.00
- Also at 116, rue du Château 75014 Paris. Open Tuesday to Friday 10.00–19.00, Saturday 10.00–19.00. Métro: Pernety
- www.pmw.fr

Jigsaws made to order

Create the jigsaw puzzle of your dreams from a cherished photo: that was the inspired idea of Michèle Wilson, who started this workshop, the only one of its kind in France, back in 1975. With its two sales outlets, one in the 14th arrondissement and the other in the 15th, this shop makes jigsaws to order from your own photos or other pictures.

The business will tackle anything. Sophie Ollé, the present owner who took over in 1997, relates: "We regularly produce invitation cards, but we've also cut up a banknote at the request of a man who was indebted to a woman but, not wanting to give her money because that's not the done thing, he thought of sending her a note in the form of a puzzle instead. Another chap had just bought a house, and to tell his wife, he gave her a jigsaw picture of it. Another one was made from an ultrasound scan …"

All the puzzles produced here are handmade, in the traditional way. What's more, the craftsmen in this 15th arrondissement shop work in front of the customers. Using a little jigsaw, they cut the card into shapes they determine themselves – in difficult puzzles, for example, they tend to follow the borders between different colours, thus confusing those who rely on the coloured areas to complete the picture.

Each jigsaw is unique. "Our 250-piece puzzles are just as complicated and entertaining as 1,000-piece factory-made ones," explains Sophie Ollé.

Another point of interest is sure to make you love this place: other than made-to-order puzzles, their main business is cutting up reproductions of works of art. Thus copies of Van Gogh's Irises pass under the saw and end up in a hundred pieces. "In reconstituting the painting, you'll discover a host of details."

It takes three weeks for a made-to-order puzzle: €36 for 80 pieces (photo 10 cm by 15 cm), €110 for 250 pieces (photo 20 cm by 25 cm). Only the two sizes are available.

POISSONNERIE LA CRIÉE DU PHARE

69, rue Castagnary 75015 Paris
- Métro: Plaisance or Porte-de-Vanves
- Tel: 01 45 31 15 00
- www.lacrieeduphare.com
- Fishmonger's open Tuesday to Thursday 9.00–13.00, Friday 9.00–13.00 and 15.30–19.00, Saturday 9.00–19.00, Sunday 9.00–13.00

A real Breton lighthouse in Paris

No, it's not just the Eiffel Tower that guides aircraft and tourists lost on their way into the city. Since 1996, an authentic lighthouse from Brittany protects Parisians near Montparnasse station. Over 10 m high, the lighthouse was towed all the way from its home region to the French capital. French and Breton flags fly at its top, and on its rear face, visible therefore only to travellers taking the train to Brittany, is written: "Gloire aux marins-pêcheurs" [Glory unto fishermen].

In fact this lighthouse is an immense advertisement to the glory of a fishmonger's shop, La Criée du Phare. This truly Parisian institution has been recently renovated and its 1,000 m² of floor space now presents a wide variety of fish, shellfish and crustaceans, as well as fruit, vegetables, flowers and wine, all at unbeatable prices. Each week four or five seafood products (among the 150 types on offer) are promoted at the lowest prices on the market: a bargain not to be missed!

As well as being the city's biggest fishmonger, it also has an extremely unusual decor.

CODINA

24, rue Violet 75015 Paris
- Métro: Charles-Michel
- Tel: 01 45 78 88 88
- Fax: 01 45 78 88 80
- Open 10.00–19.00 Monday to Saturday
- www.codina.net

Make your own soap

Specializing in 100% organic essential oils and vegetable oils, every week Codina offers workshops organized by a master soap maker who will teach you to concoct your own product. This costs €45 for a two-hour lesson, to which you should add around €23.50 for the basic ingredients. Codina's recipes are only available in its workshop. However, each student can take their soap home. Children under 14 can take part in special courses where caustic soda is replaced by a less dangerous block of glycerin.

Besides these lessons, which will appeal to children as well as curious parents, the other attraction is the oldest oil press in Paris, standing at the shop entrance.

CANINE COOKIES
MON BON CHIEN
12, rue Mademoiselle 75015 Paris • Métro Commerce
• Tel: 01 48 28 40 12 • monbonchien@yahoo.com
• Open Tuesday to Saturday 10.30–20.00 with no break

Newly arrived from Seattle with her dog Sophie, Harriet brought with her a very American concept: cookies for dogs. When you enter the shop there's no mistaking the smell: a load of cookies have just come out of the oven in the back shop. They join the dozens of others already laid out on heart-shaped plates, displayed in the window at muzzle height. On today's menu are dog biscuits with foie gras, peanut butter, carob (a substitute for chocolate, which dogs can't digest), chicken, bacon, vegetables, ginger, garlic and cheese, or beef (€10–€25 each). Plump Sophie has tried them all for sure. When first-time buyers hesitate, Harriet, a former pastry chef, gets them to taste her goodies themselves. A little dry, of course – but OK for human consumption. No sugar, no salt, no preserving agents, they are particularly good for your canine friend. Once the tasting is over, there are more surprises in store for customers – Harriet, not a woman to let herself be beaten by "French" scepticism, didn't come over from the United States empty handed. Her shop sells a range of US-made unusual gadgets and objects for dogs: nail varnish (€7), dressing gowns (€17), sweets to stop bad breath, lollies (€2.50), Catopoly (Monopoly for cats), birthday cakes (€10, with your pet's name). But Harriet's best find is a talking cushion: "Record a message and your pet will hear you talking all day long".

ANTIQUHAIR ROBY JOFFO

4, rue du Laos 75015 Paris
- Métro: Cambronne
- Tel: 01 43 06 80 16
- Portable: 06 07 87 39 27
- Open Tuesday to Saturday 10.00–18.30, with or without appointment
- www.robyjoffo.com

A haircut in an antique shop

On the fringes of the Champ de Mars, in the chic residential district of the 15th arrondissement bordering on the 7th, Roby Joffo, nephew of the celebrated French writer (Joseph Joffo et son sac de billes)* in 1994 opened his droll little establishment, half barber shop, half antique shop. Whether you're interested in clocks, antique guns or stringed instruments, or whether you'd like a haircut, you'll certainly have a good time at the great Roby's place.

Pushing fifty now, he'll tell you about his childhood in Montmartre, or details of the barbers' trade handed down by the Joffos from father to son. You'll often see a local child come in for a guitar lesson with the proud Monsieur Joffo, or an impromptu jam session between friends, all taking place among the books, the Texan armchairs in horn and cowhide, the scissors and shampoos and countless other objects of curiosity.

A dry haircut costs from €20 and the guitars between €100 and €10,000.

*The adventures of the author and his brother making their way through Occupied France during the Second World War.

A CLAIRVOYANT WHO READS CHIPS AND COUSCOUS!!

MADAME MAGDA

3, rue de l'Avre 75015 Paris
- Métro: La Motte-Picquet-Grenelle
- Tel: 01 45 79 00 13
- By appointment

This extraordinary clairvoyant will read your fortune in all kinds of things: chocolate, water, couscous, tea, champagne, even chips! Born in Bulgaria and raised in Turkey, Madame Magda is a divine (as well as divining) character, very popular on television. She receives her clients in a small apartment on rue de l'Avre.

VOITURIUM

68, avenue de Versaille 75016 Paris
• Métro: Mirabeau
• Tel: 01 42 88 51 88
• By appointment
• www.levoiturium.fr

*Hire
a classic car
to impress
your friends*

A veritable casting agency for cars, Voiturium has 5,000 vehicles on its books, representing all styles and periods (1900 to present). From Cadillacs to Clio Lambdas, via a vintage Renault 4L, you can hire almost all of them (€500 per day). For a young girl's funeral there's a pink hearse, and for a marriage the classic chauffeur-driven Cadillac, while for birthdays some people prefer the New York taxi.

If you too possess an endangered species of vehicle, don't hesitate to add it to their list, because the hiring can be done in both directions. Fees negotiable. Although the service is available to individuals, many customers are actually cinema, advertising or video-clip professionals. The Voiturium regularly supplies box-office hits. The strong point of the shop near pont Mirabeau is that it's the only one of its kind in the city. Films it has contributed to include *Podium*, *La Vérité si je mens [Would I Lie to You?]*, *Le Choix des armes [Choice of Arms]*, *Chouchou*, *Les Brigades du Tigre*, *La Bande à Bonnot [Bonnot's Gang]*, and more recently *Jet Set* and *101 Dalmatians*.

LUXURY BAGS FOR RENT ON THE INTERNET

Since April 2007, carrying this season's "IT bag" on your arm is no longer a sweet but unaffordable dream. Three different internet sites have just launched a concept that has never been tried before in France: weekly or monthly hire of designer bags from some of the biggest names in fashion. The idea is simple: you choose from among a hundred prestigious models on offer, the prices varying by category (from a modest €14 per week for a Yves Saint Laurent purse to a hefty €250 per week for the notorious Birkin from Hermès), you place your order, and 48 hours later, it's at your door, ready to go out ...
www.sacdeluxe.fr
www.feelchic.fr
www.sacdunjour.com

BACCARAT

11, place des Etats-Unis 75116 Paris
- Métro: Iéna or Boissière
- Tel: 01 40 22 11 22
- E-mail: maisonbaccarat@baccarat.fr
- www.baccarat.fr
- Shop open Monday to Friday 10.00–21.00 and Saturday 10.00–19.00
- Museum with entry fee (€7) open daily except Tuesday and Sunday, 10.00–18.30

Crystal and concrete

Since October 2003, Viscountess Marie-Laure de Noailles' extremely chic former private mansion in the north of the 16th arrondissement has been the new headquarters of the house of Baccarat. Like Madame de Noailles, an extravagant and visionary patron of the arts (she financed films by Bunuel, Cocteau and Man Ray, collected Mondrian and supported Dali), Baccarat gave a free hand to designer Philippe Starck to entirely revamp the 3,000 m² building constructed in 1895.

As soon as they step inside, visitors are overwhelmed by the very strong contrasts: the disproportionately large furnishings (including a mirrored table 14 m long and a 2,5 m monumental armchair), the delicate crystal (sumptuous chandeliers, tableware, luxury accessories), and the bare grey concrete walls, together creating an atmosphere somewhere between surreal and fairyland. Take your time to wander around the succession of rooms filled with crys-

tal, then go up to the first floor to the gallery-museum and its incredible canvas canopy painted by Garouste.

Well heeled customers will take lunch (if they've booked!) in Le Cristal Room restaurant, and in the same spirit won't be able to resist a black crystal chandelier reconstructed by Starck (€43,500), a chess set in gilded bronze and crystal (€138,000) or a punchbowl with ladle and 12 glasses (€320,000!).

To recover from the shock, stop off at the toilets on the first floor: the play of mirrors reflecting into infinity is particularly disturbing (see Paris Secret Bars and Restaurants in this series of guidebooks)

Baccarat offers a very different image from that of traditional wedding lists or grandmother's set of crystal glasses …

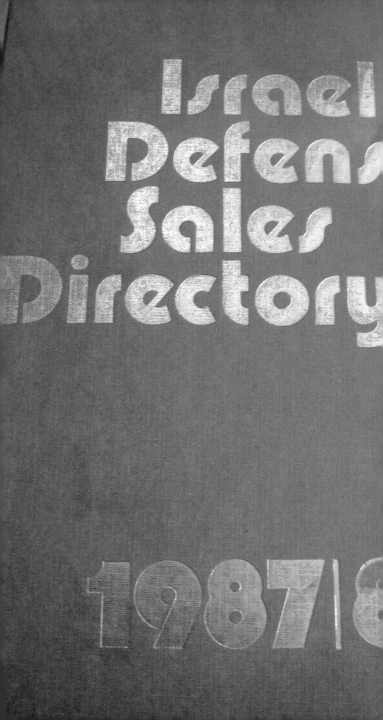

Israel Defens Sales Directory

1987/8

S.E.C.R.E.T.S

207, boulevard Péreire 75017 Paris
- Métro: Porte-Maillot
- Tel: 01 44 09 81 77
- Fax: 01 40 68 97 74
- Open Tuesday to Friday 10.00–12.30 and 14.00–18.30, Saturday 10.00–12.30
- www.barril.fr

> **As long as there are threats, there will be protection**

The name leaves no room for doubt. The Security Action Store is obviously meant for security professionals. But in fact it's the only shop in Paris that sells police and professional "equipment" to the general public.

No need to identify yourself, anyone can go in and buy. Those dreaming of uniforms will be able to purchase police belts and holsters (like the real thing but without the initials PN standing for Police Nationale), handcuffs (real too), bullet-proof vests, etc.

Would-be Inspector Gadgets will find cordless invisible headsets, cameras the size of a euro coin, electroshock weapons disguised as phones, tear-gas bombs, gas masks and a heap of books on spying, protection rackets, etc. In short, just some friendly tools for the ultra-cool.

Be warned that you're not shopping just anywhere: the place belongs to a certain Monsieur Paul Barril. Ex-head of the GIGN,* his CV can be found on his website www.barril.fr, together with a full rundown about his company, the store catalogue, and one of the house slogans: "*Tant qu'il y aura des menaces, il y aura des carapaces*" [As long as there are threats, there will be protection].

*French *gendarmerie's* elite counter-terrorism and hostage rescue unit.

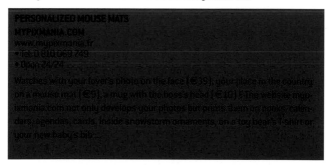

KIETUD'

5 bis, passage Doisy 75017 Paris
• Métro: Étoile
• Tel: 01 44 09 70 70
• Open Monday to Saturday 10.00–22.00, Sunday by appointment
• www.kietud.com
• €55 first session, €80 thereafter

*Isolate
yourself
in a flotation
chamber*

Let go and allow yourself to be led along. That's the only thing you need to do in this anti-stress "centre for soothing the body and mind". For that purpose, Kietud has three isolation or "flotation" chambers.

The large box-like chamber, very Seventies in its design, is filled with salt water (or a similar solution). As in the Dead Sea, your body floats by itself with no contact with the sides of the chamber.

"The absence of gravity leads to total physical and mental relaxation," explains our Zen guide. And it works! All you need do is lie down to begin tranquilly floating. The door is closed. There's no feeling of claustrophobia because some light filters through to you.

A Satie piano piece feeds through the speakers, turned very low, for the first 10 minutes. Then you totally forget yourself. This is what our hosts refer to more discreetly as sensory deprivation. You no longer really know where you are, as if in a foetal state, some say. Why not? In any case, after an hour, when the Satie comes on again, you gently come to your senses with the impression of having slept for hours. And you're now in fine form.

KATA

34, boulevard Barbès et 9, rue des Poissonniers 75018 Paris
• Métro: Barbès-Rochechouart
• No phone number
• Open Monday to Saturday 10.30–19.00

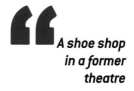

*A shoe shop
in a former
theatre*

Seen from outside, the store really doesn't look like much. Or rather it looks just like any of the innumerable bargain shoe shops on boulevard Barbès. Slippers and moccasins for €10 in the storefront window, and the atmosphere of a supermarket with floor-to-ceiling mirrors lining a corridor … Making your way through the store, however, the setting suddenly changes and you find yourself in a former theatre, perfectly preserved. The contrast is obviously very great between this place, which has retained a certain grandeur, and the bargain-basement goods on sale.

On stage, in the orchestra pit and on the balcony the stock is on display,

consisting of huge and overflowing cardboard boxes. You stroll around the rest of the orchestra pit, hunting for bargains: from €5 to €15, you'll find everything. New shoes (not always in good condition) and some designer labels (Bocage) even if the styles are clearly four or five seasons out of date. The house also has its own label. Children's styles are quite interesting: always between €5 and €15, and if you look closely you can find rather attractive Mod 8 and Aster shoes.

Warning: Credit cards are not accepted.

LIVE POULTRY FOR SALE

42, rue Myrha 75018 Paris
- Métro: Château-Rouge
- Tel: 01 46 06 46 04
- Open daily 9.00–19.00
- €15 per chicken

First catch your chicken

In the Goutte-d'Or district (named after a white wine that Henri IV was fond of ...), you'll hardly be surprised to find traders with goods aimed mainly for the local population of the neighbourhood. In one typical street a selection of table birds (hens, chickens, coqs blancs, turkeys, guinea fowl) are packed into cages. Twenty in each, explains the salesman.

Local residents prepare the birds at home in the halal tradition. They must be killed by hand, according to the decrees of the Koran, and facing Mecca.

There is another shop in Paris (quais de la Mégisserie) that sells live birds, but they are at least €50 each. Just so you know, its clientele tends to be quite different and usually have no intention of buying the birds for eating ...

HALAL MEAT

The word *halal* ("lawful") is used to designate foodstuffs authorized by Islam as opposed to those that are forbidden. For meat to be certified as halal, the animal must have had its throat cut with a single stroke of the knife and ritually bled, in the name of God. It must also be hung upside down, facing Mecca, to allow the maximum of blood to flow from the carcass (the blood representing the soul).

For those seeking greater understanding between different peoples, halal meat is technically not very different from Jewish kosher ("fit" or "proper") meat ...

SURROUND YOUR BODY WITH GIANT BUBBLES

BONJOUR L'ARTISTE

35, rue des Trois-Frères 75018 Paris • Métro: Abbesses
- Tel: 01 42 51 44 53 • www.bonjour-artiste.com
- Open Monday to Saturday 14.00–18.00

Here, in this shop devoted to the circus (there are two in Paris, the other being in rue du Cherche-Midi), you'll find a giant bubble machine imported from the United States (€20). The process is simple: soak the device in a mixture of water and washing-up liquid (you can also add glycerin), and pull the lever gently towards you. The more skilful operators will manage to surround their body with a gigantic bubble.

A tip to magicians: The shop only sells books on magic tricks to professionals. To avoid letting the rabbit out of the hat. And that's not negotiable.

CAFÉ AU LIT

16, rue de la Liberté 75019 Paris
- Métro: Danube
- Tel: 01 46 36 18 85
- http://cafeaulit.com
- Booking required

*Sleep
in an art
gallery*

For your next weekend in Paris, instead of going to a hotel, rent an art gallery in the east of the city. Café au Lit is indeed both a modern apartment and an exhibition space.

The apartment side of things is furnished for two people and equipped with a fridge and dishwasher. It costs €100 a night, three nights minimum stay. A weekend is €250, including bed linen, towels and cleaning service. Very well located in the charming Mouzaïa district, it may still seem rather out of the way if you want to stroll around the city centre.

On the gallery side, Café au Lit shows modern art with an emphasis on photography. The artists are mainly from France and Germany.

The two activities (rental and exhibition) work perfectly together thanks to a cunning arrangement designed by Didier Fiuza Faustino, who reconciles "public space and private space": the bathroom, kitchen and bedroom are all assembled on a neoprene platform. But this same platform can also serve as table, chair or bench …

So visitors can just pretend to be collectors inviting a bunch of friends over to see their latest acquisitions.

In reality, the only time a crowd does come round is on opening nights … Occupants are then asked to hide their socks and other personal effects!

JL CHAUSSURES

32, rue de la Mare 75020 Paris
• Métro: Ménilmontant or Pyrénées
• Tel: 01 43 66 03 84 (phone first for entry code)
• Open Monday to Thursday 8.30–12.00 and 13.00–18.00

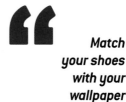

*Match
your shoes
with your
wallpaper*

Hidden away in a small back street in the Ménilmontant neighbourhood, the women's footwear workshop run by Germaine is extraordinary. The setting is particularly picturesque: the glazed workshop at the rear of a little flower garden has remained unchanged since it was set up in 1962.

Yet it would be a shame to just admire the unusual location: the footwear produced by Germaine is of very high quality. Several top designers are aware of this and have commissioned her enthusiastic team to make shoes for them.

Another peculiarity is that JL Chaussures specializes in shoes made from fabric. Although the range of models is fairly limited (shoes for weddings, ceremonies, cocktails and evenings), the choice of materials and colours is virtually endless as it's you the customer who brings your own fabric. After a presentation of the workshop's creations, you then design your own according to taste: height and width of heel, rounded, pointed or square toes, open-toed or closed, accessories (paste jewellery, lace, etc.). If you're at all worried about this, Germaine's team, headed by the adorable Gaël, will guide you, in case your legendary good taste temporarily deserts you. A pair of shoes costs on average €160 and delivery takes about fifteen days.

The house also makes leather shoes in classic colours, as well as magnificent made-to-measure boots in either fabric or leather.

A truly magical address.

SIGHTS NEARBY

ART FROM YOGURT POTS, BUTTONS, COAT HANGERS, CDS AND SHOEHORNS
EVELYNE
240, rue des Pyrénées 75020 Paris
• Métro: Pelleport
• Tel: 01 46 36 47 65
• Open Monday to Saturday 10.00–13.00 and 14.00–18.00

Behind its flamboyantly kitsch façade, Evelyne stocks some very poetic works. The artist and owner of the shop is Evelyne herself, quite a character. Her creations use quantities of buttons and coat hangers, sometimes yogurt pots, CDs, shoehorns and other oddments, which she arranges to form pictures that reflect a fantastic universe. A nod in the direction of Marcel Duchamp's irresistible "ready-mades"?

ATELIER-BOUTIQUE LES BRICOLEUSES

281, rue des Pyrénées 75020 Paris
- Métro: Jourdain or Pyrénées
- www.lesbricoleuses.com
- Open Wednesday to Sunday 15.00–20.00;
  by appointment: 06 98 46 95 66 (Emmanuelle)
- www.lesbricoleuses.com

Like going to a close friend's house

The concept of Les Bricoleuses is both original and appealing: a residence-boutique that also serves as workshop office and exhibition space. At the start, Emmanuelle, the bricoleuse [handywoman] who lives here, invited five of her friends – all creators in various media and keen on recycling materials – to show their work at her place during the open day for artists' workshops in the Belleville neighbourhood of Paris. It proved such a success that they repeated the experience, taking over the flat twice a year for brief exhibitions. But it was not until December 2004 that Emmanuelle's home, a former shoemaker's workshop, was transformed into a real boutique.

So it is now from here that this young woman sells the work of various artists, in addition to the creations of her sister bricoleuses. She selects the objects – all unique pieces – mainly following her own instincts: clothing, lamps, jewellery, accessories, furniture, paintings, photos, sculptures … and then she stocks them in her living room, kitchen, bathroom and even bedroom, which is also used as a fitting room. The prices are very reasonable, €2 for a little customized badge, €20 for a T-shirt, and €250 for a "dream box" (a ravishing box that unfolds to allow a dream universe to emerge).

Les Bricoleuses also present themselves as a sort of neighbourhood collective, and their hostess regularly rearranges her (very modular) space for a

play, photo exhibition or short film show. In March 2007, these six smashing young women also launched a new fanzine that's slightly deranged but full of hot tips and good humour.

This place really is worth a detour. Going to Les Bricoleuses is a bit like visiting a friend: you're greeted with kindness and affection, you rummage around, you get talking, and you wind up spending hours there …

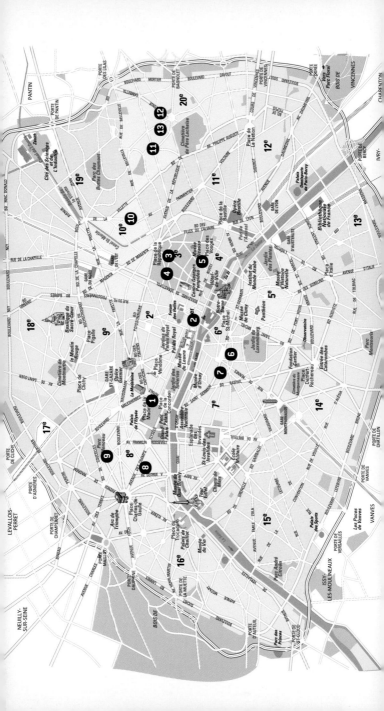

DESIGNERS

A MARVEL OF BEAUTIFUL DESIGN
Comme des Garçons ❶
54, rue du Faubourg-Saint-Honoré 75001 Paris • Tel: 01 53 30 27 27 • See page 10

HAVE A SIESTA WHILE YOU'RE SHOPPING
La Bulle Kenzo ❷
1, rue du Pont-Neuf 75001 Paris • Tel: 01 73 04 20 04 • www.labullekenzo.com
See page 24

YOUNG DESIGNER AT HOME
Martin Grant ❸
10, rue Charlot 75003 Paris • Tel: 01 42 71 39 49 • www.martingrantparis.com
See page 28

BUYING SHOES IN A FLAT
Mademoiselle Rose création ❹
4, rue Fontaine du Temple 75003 Paris • Tel: 01 48 04 55 59
• www.mademoisellerose.com • See page 38

HAVE YOUR FAVOURITE SHOES COPIED
La Boutique Sentimentale ❺
14, rue du Roi-de-Sicile 75004 Paris • Tel: 01 42 78 84 04 • See page 46

A VERTICAL GARDEN
Marithé + François Girbaud ❻
7, rue du Cherche-Midi 75006 Paris • Tel: 01 53 63 53 63 • See page 52

WEDDING GOWNS MADE FROM PAPER
The paper dresses of Mireille Etienne-Brunel ❼
37, rue de Grenelle 75007 Paris • Tel: 01 45 48 26 13 • See page 72

LIGHT IN THE DARKNESS
The black lift of magasin Louis Vuitton ❽
101, avenue des Champs-Élysées 75008 Paris • Tel: 01 53 57 52 00 • See page 78

TAILORING FOR ALL THE FAMILY UNDER ONE ROOF
216 Rivoli - Véronique des Rotours ❾
38, rue de Courcelles 75008 Paris • Tel: 01 40 08 00 20 • See page 80

A STYLIST WHO USES ONLY REMNANTS
Des Habits et Vous ❿
22, rue Jean-Moinon 75010 Paris • Tel: 01 40 18 91 66 • See page 96

MATCH YOUR SHOES WITH YOUR WALLPAPER
JL Chaussures ⓫
32, rue de la Mare 75020 Paris • Tel: 01 43 66 03 84 • See page 136

ART FROM YOGURT POTS, BUTTONS, COAT HANGERS, CDS AND SHOEHORNS
Evelyne ⓬
240, rue des Pyrénées 75020 Paris • Tel: 01 46 36 47 65 • See page 137

LIKE GOING TO A CLOSE FRIEND'S HOUSE
Atelier-boutique Les Bricoleuses ⓭
281, rue des Pyrénées 75020 Paris • Tél: 06 98 46 95 66 • See page 138

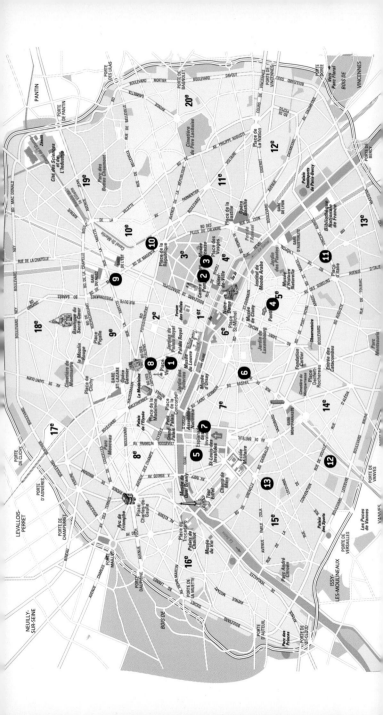

SNACKS / FOOD

JEAN-CHARLES ROCHOUX
Chocolatier
Paris

COUTANCIE BEEF
Boucherie Barone
❶

6, rue du Marché-Saint-Honoré 75001 Paris • Tel: 01 42 61 01 77
See page 12

WILLY-SHAPED BAGUETTES
Le Gay Choc
❷

45, rue Sainte-Croix-la-Bretonnerie 75004 Paris • Tel: 01 48 87 56 88
• Baguette magique 2,20 €
See page 47

SWEETS WITH A PICTURE OF THE POPE
Litchi
❸

4, rue des Écouffes 75004 Paris • Tel: 01 44 59 39 09 • www.litchi.com
See page 48

ROSE-SHAPED ICES
Gelati d'Alberto
❹

45, rue Mouffetard 75005 Paris • Tel: 01 77 11 44 55
See page 50

OFFER A CHOCOLATE RING, HEDGEHOG OR HORSE
Michel Chaudun
❺

149, rue de l'Université 75007 Paris • Tel: 01 47 53 74 40
See page 74

CHOCOLATE SCULPTURES
Chocolats Rochoux
❻

16, rue d'Assas 75006 Paris • Tel: 01 42 84 29 45
See page 75

CHOCOLATE BOUQUETS!
Le Fleuriste du chocolat
49, avenue de la Bourdonnais 75007 Paris • www.lefleuristeduchocolat.com
See page 75

❼

HONEY FROM THE OPERA BEES
Boutique de l'Opéra Garnier
8, rue Scribe 75009 Paris • Tel: 01 40 01 24 08
See page 87

❽

BEAUJOLAIS JELLY, OR JAM WITH SWEET PEPPER, COURGETTE, WALNUT AND CINNAMON
◀ Le Furet Tanrade
63, rue de Chabrol 75010 Paris • Tel: 01 47 70 48 34
See page 94

❾

YOUR PICTURE ON A BIRTHDAY CAKE
Le Gâteau doré
27 bis, rue du Faubourg-du-Temple 75010 Paris • Tel: 01 48 03 06 82
See page 97

❿

CUSTARD APPLE OR GINGER CARAMEL ICE CREAM
Glacier La Tropicale
180, boulevard Vincent-Auriol 75013 Paris • Tel: 01 42 16 87 27
See page 109

⓫

A REAL BRETON LIGHTHOUSE IN PARIS
Poissonnerie La Criée du phare
69, rue Castagnary 75015 Paris • Tel: 01 45 31 15 00
See page 116

⓬

CANINE COOKIES
Mon Bon Chien
12, rue Mademoiselle 75015 Paris • Tel: 01 48 28 40 12
See page 119

⓭

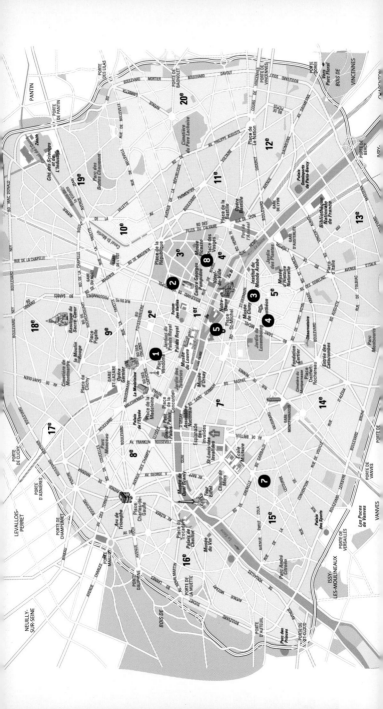

DOGS / CATS

DRESS YOUR DOG AS FATHER CHRISTMAS
Waaf et Miaou ❶
14, avenue de l'Opéra 75001 Paris • Tel: 01 42 60 02 26 • Fax : 01 42 60 02 47
See page 20

THE FIRST CRÈCHE FOR DOGS
Canicrèche ❷
32, rue de Turbigo 75003 Paris • Tel: 01 42 71 59 09 • www.canicreche.fr
See page 32

A CAT TO SUIT EVERYONE
Chat Bada ❸
23 bis, rue des Écoles 75005 Paris • Tel: 01 43 54 27 86
See page 50

CAT EXCHANGE
L'Atelier-Galerie ❹
218, rue Saint-Jacques 75005 Paris
See page 51

GIVE YOUR DOG A TREAT: OFFER IT A MASSAGE
Pinceloup ❺
53, quai des Grands-Augustins 75006 Paris • Tel: 01 44 41 14 74 • www.pinceloup.fr
See page 64

ANIMAL PORTRAITS-PHOTOS
Studio Star two two - Patrick Jullien ❻
Tel : 06 03 03 70 07 • www.patrick-jullien.com
See page 67

CANINE COOKIES
Mon Bon Chien ❼
12, rue Mademoiselle 75015 Paris • Tel: 01 48 28 40 12
See page 119

A TUXEDO FOR YOUR DOG
Un chien dans le Marais ❽
35 bis, rue du Roi-de-Sicile 75004 Paris • Tel: 01 42 74 30 06
• www.unchiendanslemarais.com

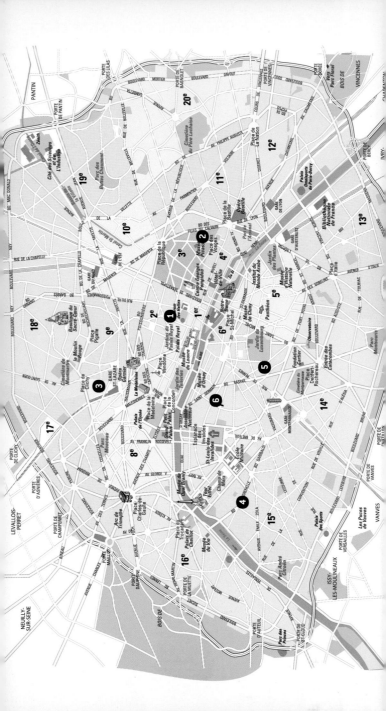

HAIRDRESSERS

HAIRDRESSER OF THE FULL MOON
Maachi Djelani

40, rue Coquillière 75001 Paris • Tel/Fax : 01 42 33 57 47 • www.lookmachine.com
See page 21

AN OLD-FASHIONED CLOSE SHAVE
ALAIN, MASTER BARBER

8, rue Saint-Claude 75003 Paris • Tel: 01 42 77 55 80
See page 40

HOME HAIRDRESSING
La Nouvelle Athènes

1, rue de Liège 75009 Paris • Tel: 01 48 74 86 89 • Mail :contact@sylviecoudray.com
• From €60 per cut
See page 84

A HAIRCUT IN AN ANTIQUE SHOP
Antiquhair Roby Joffo
❹
4, rue du Laos 75015 Paris • Tel: 01 43 06 80 16 • Portable : 06 07 87 39 27
• www.robyjoffo.com
See page 120

TWO CHILDREN'S HAIRCUTTERS WHO HAVE ADAPTED THEIR SALONS TO THE SPECIAL NEEDS OF THEIR CLIENTELE: TOYS, COMIC BOOKS, ETC.
Oscar
❺
16, rue Vavin 75006 Paris • Tel: 01 53 10 08 12
• Open Monday to Saturday 10.00–18.30

Bonton
❻
82, rue de Grenelle 75007 Paris • Tel: 01 44 39 12 01
• Open Tuesday to Saturday 10.00–19.00

ALPHABETICAL INDEX

Dan Assayag

Cartography: JB Nény - **Design:** Roland Deloi - **Layout:** Stéphanie Benoit - **Copy-editing/proof-reading (original French edition):** Marielle Gaudry - **English translation:** Thomas Clegg and Caroline Lawrence - **Diffusion :** Michelin

Printed in France by MAME in july 2007. Registration of copyright july 2007.
ISBN: 978-2-9158-0721-9

© JONGLEZ 2007

Jacques Garance et Maud Ratton – Photos S. Rivoal

SECRET
PARIS

JONGLEZ

WALKING OFF THE BEATEN TRACK

A tree in a church, an atomic bomb shelter under the Gare de l'Est, a sundial designed by Dalí, a prehistoric roundabout, a solid gold sphere in the French parliament, a Chinese temple in a parking lot, the effect of the Bièvre river on Parisian geography, a blackhouse in the Bois de Boulogne, a Breton lighthouse near Montparnasse, unsuspected traces of brothels, a priest who blesses animals ...

Paris can surprise residents as well as occasional visitors on the look-out for closely guarded secrets.

UNUSUAL SHOPPING
IN PARIS

Have your hair cut on the night of the full moon, take a siesta while shopping, make a cast of your foot, top a birthday cake with your own photo, issue your own stamps, take pictures of your aura, visit a designer at home, join an art gallery open 24/24, buy shoes in a theatre, offer your cat or dog a massage or special cookies, relax in a flotation chamber, try out extraordinary Japanese toilets …

Shopping in Paris has never been so stimulating, although you have to know where to go …

As a change from traditional retailers, here are over a hundred unusual places where you can find really original presents.

JONGLEZ
16,90€

info@editionsjonglez.com
www.editionsjonglez.com

ISBN : 978-2-9158-0721-9

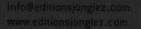

9 782915 807219